IKAT TECHNIQUE

IKAT TECHNIQUE
JACKIE BATTENFIELD

VNR VAN NOSTRAND REINHOLD COMPANY
New York Cincinnati Toronto London Melbourne

Printed in the United States of America
All photographs, unless otherwise credited, by Stephan Spera
Designed by Loudan Enterprises

Published in 1978 by Van Nostrand Reinhold Company
A division of Litton Educational Publishing, Inc.
135 West 50th Street, New York, NY 10020, U.S.A.

Van Nostrand Reinhold Limited
1410 Birchmount Road, Scarborough, Ontario M1P 2E7, Canada

Van Nostrand Reinhold Australia Pty. Limited
17 Queen Street, Mitcham, Victoria 3132, Australia

Van Nostrand Reinhold Company Limited
Molly Millars Lane, Wokingham, Berkshire, England

16 15 14 13 12 11 10 9 8 7 6 5 4 3 2 1

Library of Congress Cataloging in Publication Data

Battenfield, Jackie.
  Ikat technique.

  Bibliography: p.
  Includes index.
  1. Ikat. I. Title.
TP897.B29   746.6   77-8669
ISBN: 0-442-20595-3

Acknowledgments

I wish to thank the following people for their help in writing this book: Julie Bagish, Kristi Kolln, Nancy Sharples, "Eddie" Stirling, and Gail Martin of Artweave Textile Gallery. Bronwen Solyom graciously provided her kind support and knowledge of ikat throughout the world, past and present, to my questions and to the manuscript. My appreciation to Michael Bogle, for allowing me to excerpt and reproduce material in Appendix B from his *Textile Dyes, Finishes, and Auxiliaries* (Garland Publishing Company, New York, 1976).

My special love and thanks to Dolores Brien, who not so gently pushed me into this project, and to Ines, who had to live with me and the book during its completion.

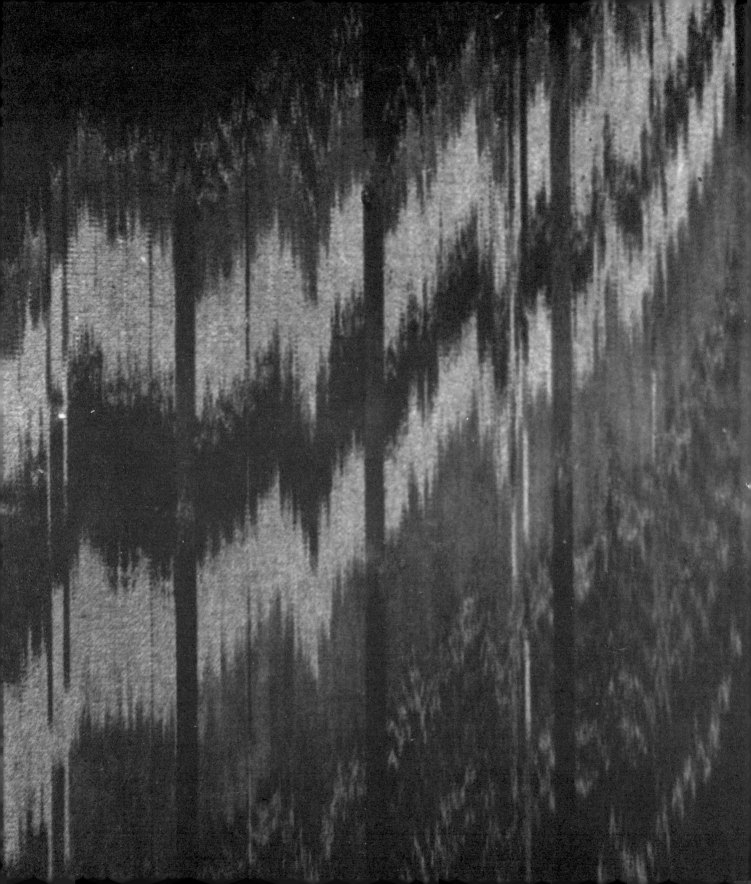

Contents

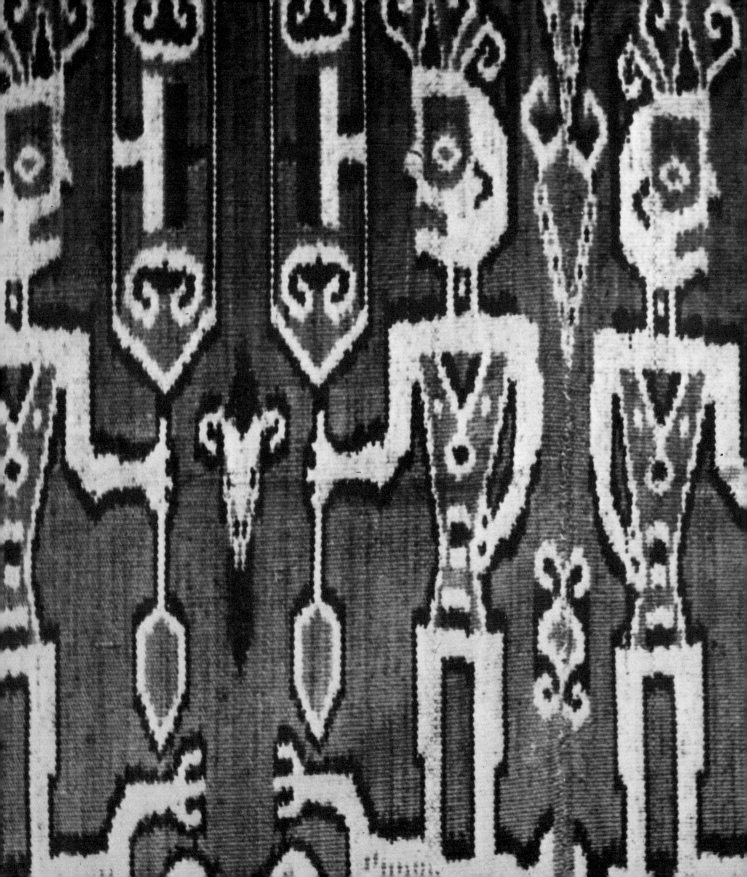

Introduction

The purpose of this book is to introduce the intermediate and the advanced weaver to ikat, a method of tie-dyeing yarns that, when woven or otherwise constructed, produces patterns with characteristically blurred edges. The book assumes that the weaver has a good grasp of the fundamentals of handweaving and is interested in experimenting with design through dyeing processes. It does not assume that the weaver has an expert knowledge of dyeing, for there are many skilled weavers today who produce excellent work but who have never attempted to dye their own yarns. Through ikat technique the fiber artist can develop dyeing skills and at the same time experiment with dyes as a design component. For this reason design, color, and dyeing are discussed as well as ikat technique itself.

As the examples included in this book suggest, ikat can be used to produce the exquisite detailed, intricate patterns typical of many traditional fabrics as well as the bold, abstract patterns favored by contemporary weavers. Making an ikat can require painstaking precision, but the technique can also be used by the weaver who is interested in chance as a factor in design.

The scope of this book is modest—to provide the weaver with a reasonably uncomplicated approach to ikat technique that nevertheless includes the essential elements of the most complex as well as the simplest of ikats.

The Ancient Art of Ikat: a Brief History

There are very few contemporary weaving and dyeing techniques that do not have a long and solid historical base. Ikat is no exception. It would be impossible to include the complete history of ikat in this chapter: the next few pages show only some of the thousands of beautiful ikats in the world, each with its own story to be told, and the cultures mentioned represent only a fraction of those that have practiced ikat in the past. My aim is to give you some background in order to whet your appetite so that you will search out your own areas of interest.

The work "ikat" is a derivative of the Malay word *mengikat*, which means "to tie," and this definition describes the process. Ikat refers to the binding and dyeing of yarns prior to weaving, the opposite of batik or plangi, which use resist methods on an already woven fabric. Ikat thus produces a variegated yarn that is woven into a prearranged pattern. Because the dye has a tendency to bleed into the areas wrapped

1-1. Lemdessar, Tarat, Tanimbar Islands, late 19th century. Sarong, lontar palm and cotton. Warp-faced plain weave with warp ikat of bast fiber. Collection of the Textile Museum of the District of Columbia. Photo courtesy of Moltz.

with the resist bindings, due primarily to capillary action along the yarn, it imparts a blurred, fuzzy edge to the pattern, which is often acccentuated during the weaving process.

It is easy to imagine the manner in which ikat may have first been discovered. A streaked bundle of fibers, when warped, might have suggested a form or pattern. Yarns may later have been kept out of the dyepot to create stripes and later still wrapped so that the patterns could be better controlled. The oldest known ikats, found in some parts of eastern Indonesia, are made of a very primitive type of material called bast, which is the unspun fiber from the bark or leaves of certain trees. Figure 1-1 shows a 19th-century sarong from Tanimbar in which bast is knotted into long fibers to form the warp-ikat stripes.

It is still not known whether the technique originated in Indonesia and spread through trade routes to the rest of the world: it may have been developed independently by several cultures, most likely in Indonesia, India, and western and eastern Asia. Whether the technique had one origin or several, it was known throughout the world at an early date.

Recent excavations in Peruvian grave sites have yielded pre-Columbian ikat fabrics. These fabrics were in existence long before the Spanish Conquest. Either knowledge of the technique was carried over through trade or by immigrants or it was developed independently. Ikat fabrics have also been found in Japan and Egypt dating back to the 6th and 8th centuries A.D., and from the Middle East from the 8th century A.D. Evidence from the 7th-century cave paintings of Ajanta indicates that resist techniques were also known in India from early times. The development of resist techniques—ikat, batik, and plangi—has been very important to Asia. While the western world was concentrating on tapestry techniques to create images and designs, this part of the world also imparted images through resists.

Ikats vary enormously in design and materials from one culture to another. One reason for the diversity is that ikats are often used for ceremonial purposes, so designs are dictated by the customs of the culture. In all cases local weaving materials and dyestuffs also make each group of ikats unique. All types of fibers have been used by various peoples to make ikats, depending upon what was available. Cotton and silk are the most widely used, linen and wool less frequently. A look at the major centers of ikat shows why this is so. For the most part they tend to be heavy cotton- and silk-producing areas. In countries in which wool and linen were used, generally cooler regions, it was found that the ikat technique also worked well with these fibers.

The different types of ikats are warp, weft, and double. They are named for the woven use of the yarn after it has undergone the resist process. Warp ikats (figure 1-2) carry the pattern only on the warp yarns; weft ikats (figure 1-3), on the weft yarns; double ikats (figure 1-4), matched patterns on both the warp and the weft. All cultures known to use this technique appear to have made warp ikats. The warp seems to be the most likely candidate for the process, since warp yarns are stretched on the loom and are more easily controlled than weft yarns. Some cultures in ancient Peru and in parts of Africa and Indonesia used warp-ikat techniques exclusively. In most cases the warp ikats were woven with a warp-faced weave, as shown in figure 1-5. This ensured the clearest image, since the plain-colored weft yarns were completely covered and did not interrupt the flow of the dyed pattern.

Some of the most beautiful ikats come from the island of Sumba in the Indonesian Archipelago. Stylized human figures and animals from myths and sacred rites fill every area of the ikat. The cloths are usually worn by noblemen or their retainers and are required for certain ceremonial dances. They are also used as marriage gifts and often accompany the deceased to the grave as a shroud. In short, possession of an ikat symbolizes wealth and status in the community. Figures 1-6 and 1-7 show a contemporary Sumba warp ikat. It is made of cotton, and birds and lions are the repeated forms. Birds such as roosters and hens have long been a part of Sumba ikat symbolism. The lion motif is an addition from the Dutch. The Dutch traded with and colonized the islands, and the lion figure was probably picked up from the Dutch coat of arms.

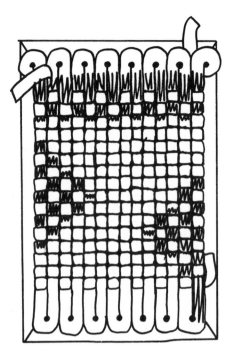

1-2. Warp ikat woven in a 50/50 weave.

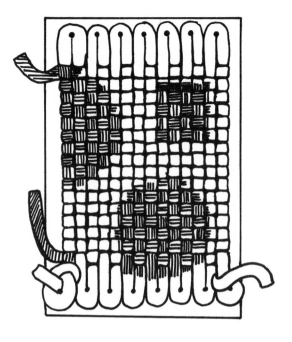

1-4. Double ikat woven in a 50/50 weave.

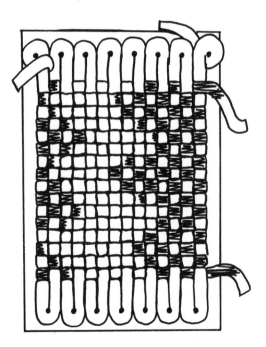

1-3. Weft ikat woven in a 50/50 weave.

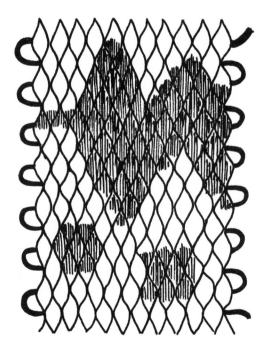

1-5. Warp-faced weave on a warp ikat. This weave gives the clearest image of the pattern.

The ikat was formed by placing four equal sections of the warp on top of each other and wrapping the pattern through all four layers. The ikat was later laid out and warped to develop the mirror image between the quarters and down the middle. Some Sumba ikats have as many as 16 sections, warped and tied at the same time, each forming a mirror image to the section next to it. Even the fringe has a striped ikat pattern. Because the designs are traditional, they are usually executed from memory or copied from another cloth. Figure C-1 shows another example of a Sumba cloth, this one from the 19th century.

1-7. Detail of Sumba cloth. Notice the mirror image created by reversing the four panels.

1-6. Sumba, Indonesia, 1958. Royal cloth, ceremonial man's sarong, cotton, warp ikat in red, blue, and white, 8½' × 4'. Collection of Artweave Textile Gallery, New York.

Figures predominate in a warp ikat from nearby Borneo (figure 1-8). This cloth is called a *pua*, which means a ceremonial hanging or cover. As in Sumba, the warps in this ikat are arranged so that the symbols form mirror images. All are human figures, some facing the viewer directly, others standing in profile. In each row the figures wear a different pattern of clothing, with the middle figures standing on what may be a fallen enemy. These ikats are also symbols of wealth, prestige, and honor.

Celebes, another island in Indonesia, is the origin of the warp ikats shown in figures 1-9 and 1-10. Unlike the other ikats discussed, these two include strong geometric shapes that form mazelike structures. These motifs may once have represented specific figures, but they have since been abstracted into geometric shapes. The ikats are woven from heavy cotton and utilize the ikat form throughout the woven surface. The pieces, which are as wide as 6', were woven in two strips and later joined in the middle, again creating a mirror image of the two halves. The ikat in figure 1-9 has an elongated triangular motif along the top and the bottom. This triangle, which points towards the edge of the ikat, is sometimes called a *tumpal* motif and is a very old geometric figure. The cut-diamond and star forms are typical of these ikats.

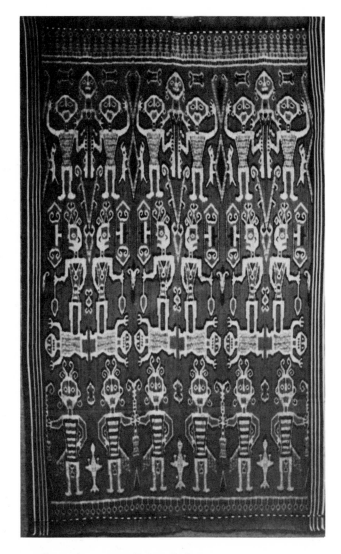

1-8. Iban tribeswomen, Borneo, Indonesia, contemporary. Ceremonial blanket (*pua*), cotton, warp ikat, 38″ × 62″. Collection of Artweave Textile Gallery, New York.

1-9. Celebes, Indonesia, 20th century. Ceremonial cloth (*sekomandi*), cotton, warp ikat, 5′ × 6′. Collection of Artweave Textile Gallery, New York.

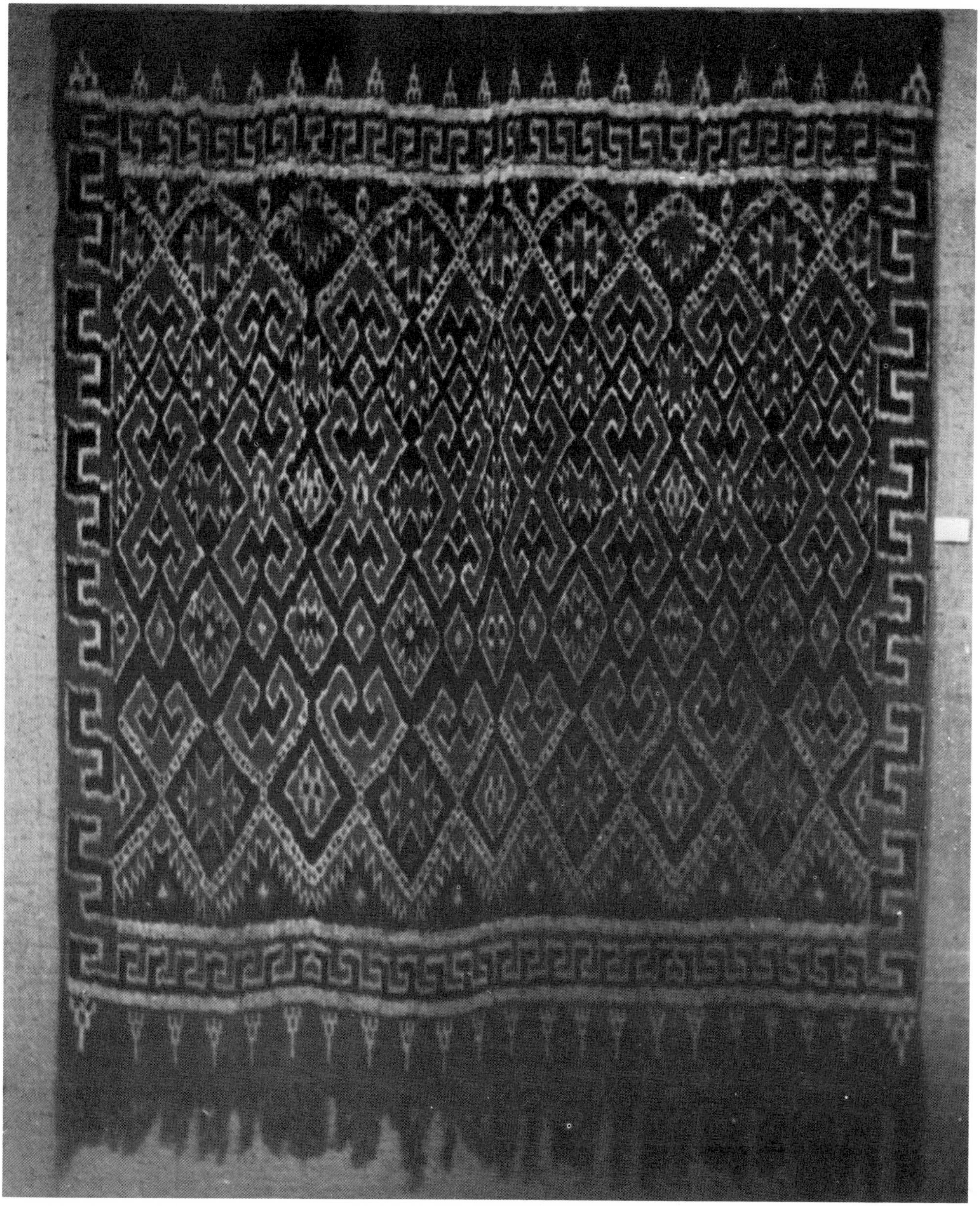

1-10. Celebes, Indonesia, early 20th century. Ceremonial cloth, cotton, warp ikat, 66″ × 100″. Collection of Artweave Textile Gallery, New York.

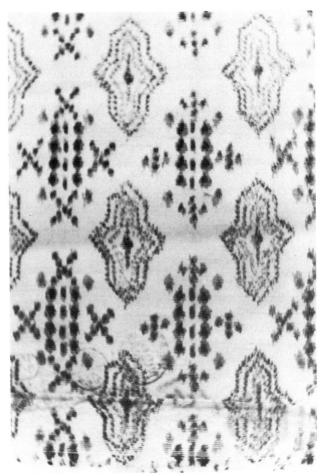

1-11. Japan, contemporary. Ikat fabric (*kasuri*), cotton, warp ikat.

1-12. Orissa, India, 19th century. Cotton weft-ikat sari, 38″ × 84″. Collection of Syracuse University, Syracuse, New York. Photo courtesy of Syracuse University.

The Japanese have developed numerous ways to create ikat—or *kasuri*—effects on fabric. The methods include wrapping threads in the traditional manner; binding the threads according to a guide thread that has been marked beforehand; squeezing the threads between hard cutout, patterned boards, using the wood contact to create the resist; and using rollers to print the patterns directly on the threads. Although the latter method is not strictly an ikat process, the visual result is similar. Figure 1-11 shows a contemporary fabric made by this method. A special

Japanese double ikat called *noto joofu* comes from the Noto Peninsula. Figure C-2 shows an example of a 40-year-old fabric in this style. This technique uses wooden blocks instead of wrapping to create the resist pattern.

India has also developed a strong ikat tradition. Resist techniques were already known over 1,300 years ago, as shown by cloths depicted in cave paintings of that time. Figure 1-12 shows part of a sari cloth from Orissa, an area along the eastern coast of India. Typical forms are sea animals. In this ikat

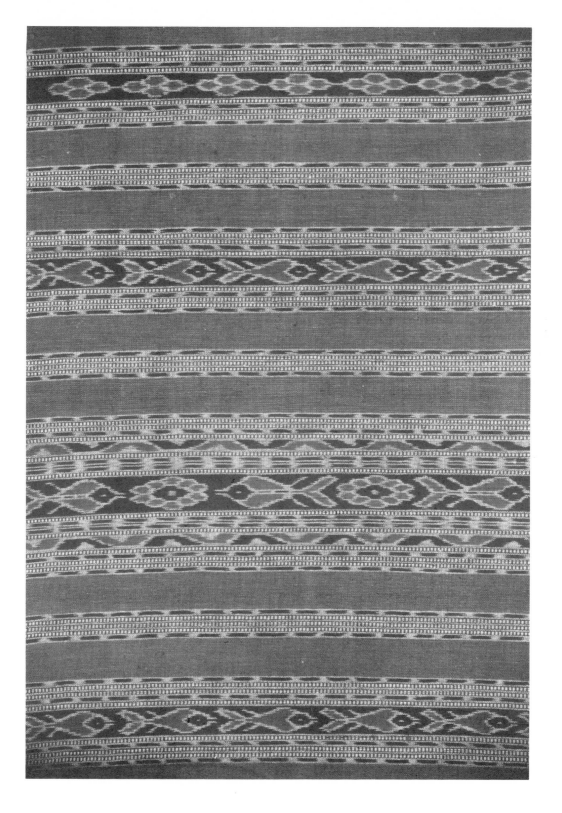

there are wide bands of fish and rosettes along with narrow bands of stripes, pulled to simulate the wavelike motion of the water. The entire pattern, although tightly structured, has a flowing sensation due to the arrangements of the narrow-striped ikat bands that outline the figurative elements of the design. The pattern is pulled into the warp after the ikat is dyed into stripes. It is the stripes tied to the loom and pulled in such a way that create diagonals and arrowheads. Figure 1-13 shows the changes that can be made in a simple striped-ikat warp by pulling the threads into new arrangements. There is some speculation that pulled patterns originated in India. Some of the most exquisite of all ikats are the silk *patolas* from Gujarat, India. These are finely detailed double ikats. Characteristically carrying lozenge and rosette patterns, elephants, and other figurative elements appear as well. Only a few families still make these beautiful ikats. Figure 1-14 shows a detail of a *patola* and illustrates the complexity of the flower pattern and the perfect craftsmanship required to match a complicated design in both the warp and the weft.

The dramatic ikats of the Uzbek in Turkistan were usually used for quilts and for ceremonial and festival robes. They are characterized by large, bold geometric patterns. These forms often represent stylized images of fruits, flowers, and other objects. Through years of abstraction the motifs have lost their meaning and have emerged as strong decorative forms. Figure 1-15 shows a 19th-century warp ikat of silk and cotton. Such cloths were often sewn together with little regard to matching patterns, creating interesting juxtapositions of large forms.

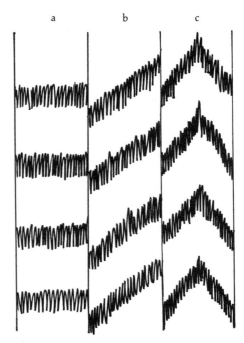

1-13. Pulled-stripe warp-ikat pattern: (a) represents the unpulled warp, (b) a diagonal pulled on one side, and (c) the arrowhead or flame pulled pattern.

1-14. India, early 19th century. Double ikat (*patola*), silk. Collection of G. W. Watters.

20

Arabian and Indian trade possibly brought ikat to Africa. Since Islam does not allow the portrayal of living forms, African ikats rely heavily on stripes and pulled forms rather than on plant and animal motifs to create the patterns. Figure 1-16 shows how strips of ikat warp are combined with plain-warp sections to create the pattern. Ikats were used for both men's and women's weaves.

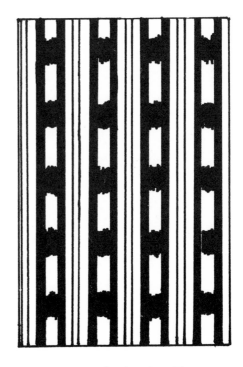

1-16. Strip ikat from East Africa.

1-15. Uzbek tribe, Turkistan, 19th century. Warp ikat, cotton weft, silk warp, 82" × 66". Collection of Artweave Textile Gallery, New York.

Ikat was once quite widely practiced in Europe. Trade with the East brought ikat cloths into Europe, where the technique was sometimes adapted to local needs and tastes. Figure 1-17 shows a pattern stick. The warp or weft was wound around the stick at either end, and grooves cut into the wood indicated where the pattern was to be wrapped. Flame patterns (pulled arrowheads) were most popular and were used for peasant costumes, silk ribbons, and fine handkerchiefs, to name a few items. Wool as well as other fibers were used. Knitting wool in England apparently underwent the ikat process, maybe a precursor of the variegated knitting yarns of today. With the advent of sophisticated machines for printing and weaving fabric the use of ikat gradually died out.

In Central and South America, as mentioned earlier, ikat was practiced before the time of Columbus. Figure 1-18 shows a pre-Columbian ikat from a Peruvian grave site at Pachcamac. The Peruvians generally wove their cotton-warp ikats in an open, gauzelike weave. Geometric patterns and a bird form appear in this ikat. Like other cultures,

1-17. A wooden pattern stick. The grooves indicate areas to be wrapped.

1-18. Pachacamac, Peru, pre-Columbian. Cotton warp-ikat fragment found at a grave site. Collection of the University Museum, University of Pennsylvania. Photo courtesy of the University Museum.

22

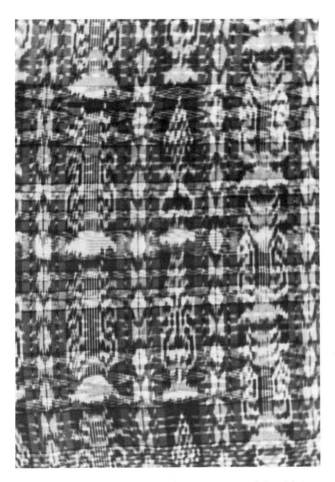

1-19. Guatemala, contemporary. Cotton, compound-ikat fabric. Collection of Michael Bogle.

the Peruvians often used figures that appeared in other crafts such as pottery. Ikat is still a thriving technique in several parts of Latin America. Peru, Chile, Ecuador, Colombia, and Central America have practiced it. Guatemala has developed a strong cottage industry in ikat, supplying enough for local needs and exporting it to other countries. Figure 1-19 shows a contemporary compound-ikat fabric. It is called compound ikat because the warp- and weft-ikat yarns are not meant to be matched into one pattern. Long ikat warps are prepared and spaced into a warp. Another ikat pattern is woven as the weft, creating a myriad of complex shapes and forms. Figure C-3 shows another example of a Guatemalan compound ikat.

Although this chapter represents only a brief overview of ikat and its history, you can see how its long tradition has extended into most sections of the world. It has always lent itself to the possibilities and needs of the craftsmen and cultures that embraced it.

Design and Color

DESIGN

Now that you have some background on ikat and are aware of the startling results that other cultures have achieved, you are ready to think about your own design. Designing an ikat is an exciting experience, for it allows you to work freely, to play with shapes and forms without being restricted—for the moment—by the warps and wefts. I take great satisfaction in the painterly effect that is achieved by dye seepage under the wrappings, which softens the color and the edge. This is an essential part of an ikat's beauty and should be exploited whenever possible.

Design is crucial to the final work. The first aspect of the weaving to be noticed, the design tempts the observer to make a closer, more careful inspection. It is the stuff that inspires serious contemplation, and for that reason it must be given very careful thought before proceeding with the work. No matter how wonderful the craftsmanship or how tactile the materials, an uninspired design makes a dull piece of work. I am amazed at how often my students seem willing to settle for the first marks that come from their pencils: lines and shapes that appear on the

paper are neither manipulated nor explored thoroughly. Designing should be one of the hardest and most time-consuming stages of the entire ikat process, as it is in any creative work. An idea can hover just short of complete consciousness for days, even months before it finally emerges. Once you have a design, the rest of the process is primarily motor movement—wrapping, dyeing, and weaving—steps that require a great deal of control and craftsmanship but little creativity. But the original idea and design? This step requires the most patience from the artist.

Sources of Designs

Everyone has an innate sense of design. Where do ideas for designs come from? Much as they do for such creative work as writing, painting, or inventing, they come from your environment and your imagination. A starting point might be the concrete objects around you—bark on a tree, flower coloration, a cityscape (figures 2-1 and 2-2). Most artists have found that certain forms appeal to them and have repeated these forms over and over in their work. Artists are identified by their subject matter and by

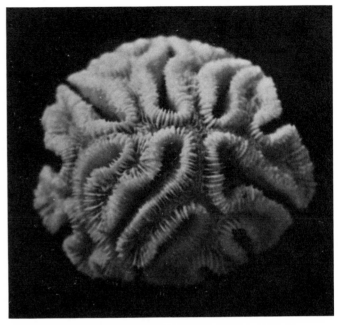

2-1. The bark of a tree is only one example of how you can use nature as a source of design.

2-2. Another source of design from nature, a piece of coral.

the characteristic ways in which it is presented. Contemporary visual arts and artists can be another source of inspiration; a written description of a person or a place may spark an idea.

The approach to the arts taken by other cultures is a valuable source of design. It may be the culture's philosophy that is most attractive and supportive of your own work (figures 2-3 and 2-4). Since ikat has its roots in eastern and Indian cultures, here are many sources of design for the contemporary artist (figures 2-5 and 2-6).

Designs and patterns in historical ikats were controlled by cultural attitudes, legends, myths, and rituals. The contemporary artist has much more freedom to explore personal as well as cultural symbolism. Because you are not tied to the traditions of ikat design, you can be as abstract, as realistic, as expressionistic, as experimental, or as controlled as

the technique allows. With this freedom the security that surrounds traditional ikat craftsmen is lost. Their designs are already laid out; yours are not. Many is the time that I've yearned to repeat a worn-out, trite design and skip the designing process. But I reject that thought after a moment, for I don't want to stop the growing and learning that results from creative thought.

No matter what the source, it is very important to keep a record of your ideas. Most artists have a small sketchbook with them at all times—even next to the bed at night—to jot down ideas or images whenever they occur. Not that all these images will find their way into a design. An image is like a dream—if it is not instantly recalled and recorded, it will often be lost forever. Keeping a diary of this sort gives you a fruitful source to go back to time and time again.

25

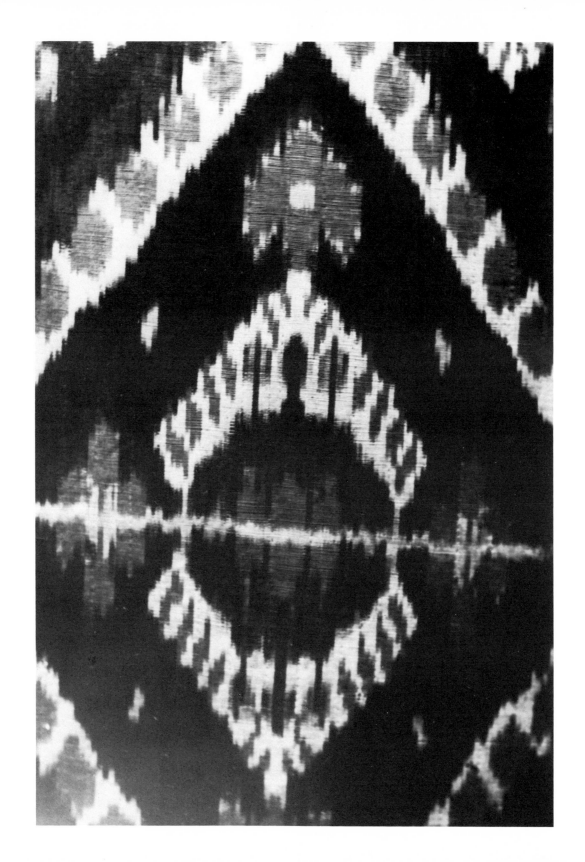

2-4. Scarf from Flores made of ikat strips. Several ikat strips can be combined to create an interplay of forms. Collection of Susan Goldin.

2-3. The geometric pattern of a 19th-century ikat from Turkistan (detail) is a historical source of design. Collection of Artweave Textile Gallery, New York.

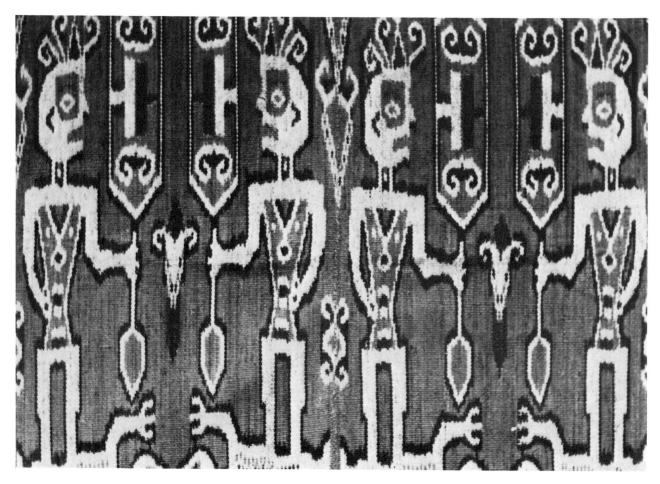

2-5. Contemporary ikat from Borneo. The profiled human figures are traditional motifs. Collection of Artweave Textile Gallery, New York.

2-6. Kay Rosenberg, untitled. Cotton, tapestry weave, 10¼" × 9¾". A contemporary ikat that utilizes the figures and mirror images of Borneo.

28

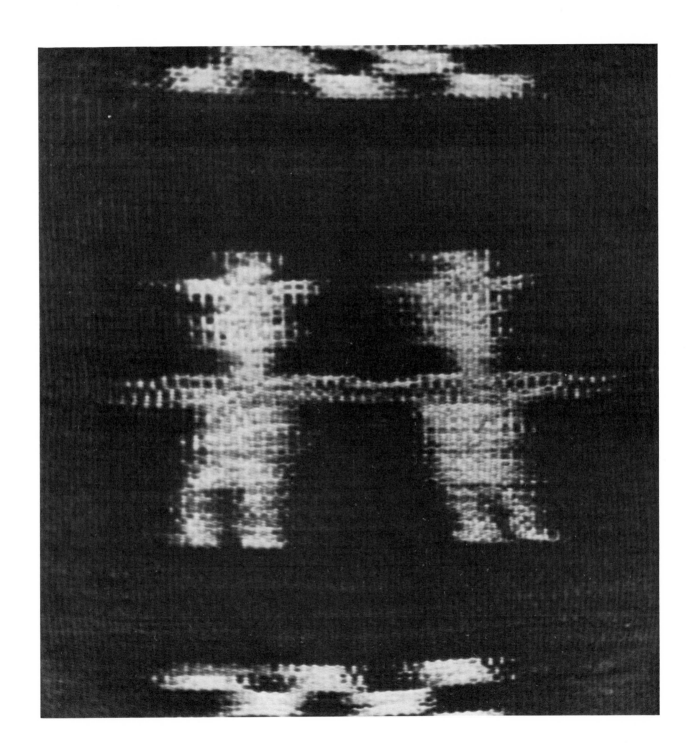

Developing a Design

Once an idea begins to take shape, draw it and redraw it several times. Stretch it. Shrink it. Rearrange the space around it. Try various color combinations. Divide a large sheet of paper into smaller compartments and draw the design 10 or more times. Stand back and see which is the most pleasing. Which one solves the problem in the best way? Which is the most exciting? Work out exact dimensions and enlarge the drawing to at least 18" x 24" if your piece is to be that size or larger. Do not work from a tiny sketch, for it may not enlarge as anticipated, and what may be graceful as a 2" design can be overwhelming if it is 4' long.

If your head seems to be spinning and nothing looks right at this stage of the process, walk away from your work and let it sit for a few hours or days. If you return to the drawing with fresh eyes and a clear mind, the most appealing design will often jump right out at you. I make it a practice to live with a design for a few days before executing it in order to test its staying power.

I cannot overemphasize the importance of not rushing these early stages. You need a strong will to live through the sometimes painful moments of creating. Everyone wants to get started with the work, but, in your rush, the end result may not be as strong as you wanted.

The intended use of the ikat is a prime factor in the design. Is it to be a wall hanging or fabric yardage? How much time can feasibly be devoted to wrapping the yarns? A complex design can require hours of wrapping yarns; others may need only a quick, simple binding and a dip into the dyebath.

A second important consideration in designing an ikat is the color. Because ikat calls for top dyeing, careful attention should be given to the compatibility of the colors in your design. It theoretically is possible to use any combination of colors, but certain choices require extra wrapping and unwrapping and careful advance planning. An otherwise beautiful design can be ruined by mismatched colors that emerge from further top dyeing. A brief review of color theory is given later in this chapter.

Ikats are characterized by blurred, indefinite edges. Because the yarns are actually "painted" with color, small details are possible. If the design calls for sharply defined edges or borders, it is obviously not suitable to ikat. (If you really want to do it, look into a tapestry technique instead.) Perfectly straight, hard-edged diagonals are also difficult to achieve. A design with a fresh calligraphic, linear quality—senseless to force into the ikat technique—calls for another resist method such as batik. The most prominent element in an ikat design is the painterly effect, due to the fuzzy outlines that run through each piece of work. It is foolish to use a technique as strong in character as ikat if you must minimize its effect in order to accommodate your design. Almost any design, however, can be interpreted in an ikat, provided that you are prepared for the final effect. Look at the cartoon and the final double ikat illustrated in figures 2-7 and 2-8. What is explicit in the cartoon becomes muted and obscure in the finished double ikat. The dramatic slashes of color and rigorous movements in the cartoon are transmuted and tamed into subtle dyed effects in the finished ikat.

2-7. Cartoon for a double ikat. Oil pastel on paper.

2-8. Double ikat loosely interpreting the cartoon. Wool, 50/50 weave.

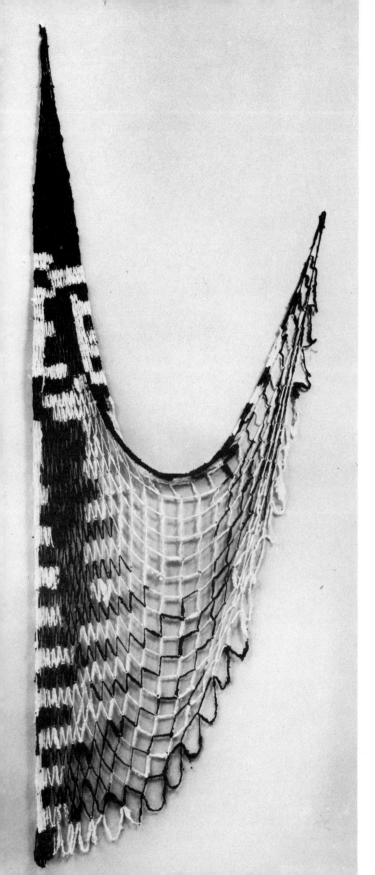

The particular ikat technique to be used is also a consideration in design. Besides warp, weft, and double ikats, as described and illustrated in the preceding chapter, there are countless other ways in which the ikat technique can be used. Plaiting and crocheting are some examples (figure 2-9). Consider for a moment the ways in which an ikat (figure 2-10) can be woven. The same design can be woven in a warp-faced tapestry weave (figure 2-11), in a 50/50 or tabby weave with a thick (figure 2-12) or thin (figure 2-13) weft, or in a 2/2 twill pattern (figure 2-14). In the tabby and the twill weaves the pattern appears disjointed and not as clear as in the tapestry weave. In the former techniques the warp only holds the fibers together: it does not appear on the surface. Considering all the weaving techniques, such as overshot patterns, twill variations, double weave, and leno technique, to name only a few, you have unlimited possibilities.

If the clearness of the design is paramount, either a warp-faced or a weft-faced ikat will give the best results. With these techniques you can be sure that the design will not get lost. Other designs may welcome a dispersion into the constrasting color of a warp or weft, and other techniques, such as those mentioned above, may be preferable. The strong vertical or horizontal movement created by bleeding in either the warp or the weft can work for or against a design.

A double ikat is the hardest to control, since both warp and weft undergo the ikat technique. If a very clear design is called for, great skill must be employed to obtain a perfect match of the two yarns. The blurring of the edges in both directions will create rounder, softer forms.

2-9. Joanne Segal Brandford, untitled, 1975. Cotton and silk, vat-dyed, knotted netting, 22′ × 56″. The lyrical sweep of the curve and the fading color take advantage of the properties of net. Photo courtesy of Hillel Burger.

2-10. Cartoon for a potential ikat design.

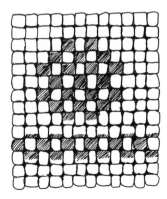

2-11. The same design as in figure 2-10 ikated into the warp yarns and woven in a warp-faced weave.

2-13. The result of using a thin weft with the same ikat-patterned warp in the same design as in figure 2-10.

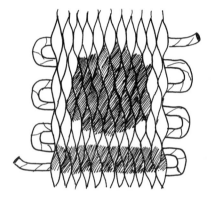

2-12. The same design as in figure 2-10 woven in a 50/50 weave.

2-14. The design in figure 2-10 woven in a 2/2 twill pattern.

The last design consideration involves the surprise factor. The fact that you cannot always be sure about the end result can become either a positive or a negative aspect of the design. It is here that the weaver must be most flexible. Change (I prefer to call it "surprise") will occur, but it can unwittingly play an integral part in your design. It may be of some consolation that these surprises may add to the design, although they take some getting accustomed to. I remember being dismayed when I unwrapped an area that I had dyed a vivid yellow and found green spots. After weaving the piece I was glad to have those spots, for they transformed what might have been an overpowering colored area into one that blended well with the rest of the piece. On the other hand, I have seen students unwrap ikats only to discover that, due to excessive seepage of dye under the wrappings, their design had disappeared! Very tight, intricately patterned ikats demand as few surprises as possible, but the ikat always has the last say, which is one of its charms.

COLOR

Designing an ikat is probably not the first occasion on which the fiber artist has grappled with colors, nor will it be the last. Because mixing colors is so important in the ikat process, a short review of the theory of color combinations may be helpful.

Today the fiber artist has a wide selection of dyes to choose from, each with a huge palette of colors and a particular method to follow. This situation is in direct contrast to traditional ikat, in which local plants supplied the colors. Craftsmen from the island of Rote, for example, were limited primarily to the colors blue (indigo), red, and yellow. These dyes had been used for many centuries, and there was little chance of poor color mixing, due to the repetition of the tradition. Even more amazing is the amount of time consumed in dyeing. You may complain about the number of hours spent on each dyebath, but in Indonesia dyeing the red alone can take as long as six months. In fact, the entire dyeing process requires at least a year, often longer. By contrast modern methods are quick and easy. Every color of the rainbow is at the disposal of today's dyer. This freedom is wonderful, but, because we are freed from a dependence upon local dyestuffs, choosing and mixing colors are very important.

Color theory has occupied the attention of artists throughout history. A basic understanding of the properties of color is a necessary and powerful tool for the artist. The speculations of Sir Isaac Newton, who postulated that white light is the combination of many colors, are the basis of much of today's color theory.

There are several approaches to the study of color, each with its own rules. Optics, which treats the color spectrum in light and its effects upon the eyes, is one way of dealing with color. In this system the primary colors are red, blue, and green, and sensors in the eyes are capable of perceiving these three colors and blending them to create all colors seen by man. In optics color is additive, since, when you see a red apple, all colors except red are absorbed by the apple and the red is reflected back into your eyes, which registers its hue.

Color theory in relation to dyestuffs is another matter. Most colorists in the past have named red, blue, and yellow as the primary colors. All other colors of the spectrum are supposedly derived from mixtures of these three. This theory has since been altered to the extent that the colors magenta (bluish red), cyan (greenish blue), and yellow are now considered primaries, since mixtures of these three yield the largest number of intense hues.

The most familiar illustration of color theory is the color wheel. This marvelously simple device for examining color properties was first drawn over 250 years ago by Sir Isaac Newton. The color wheel is traditionally divided into 12 segments (figure 2-15),

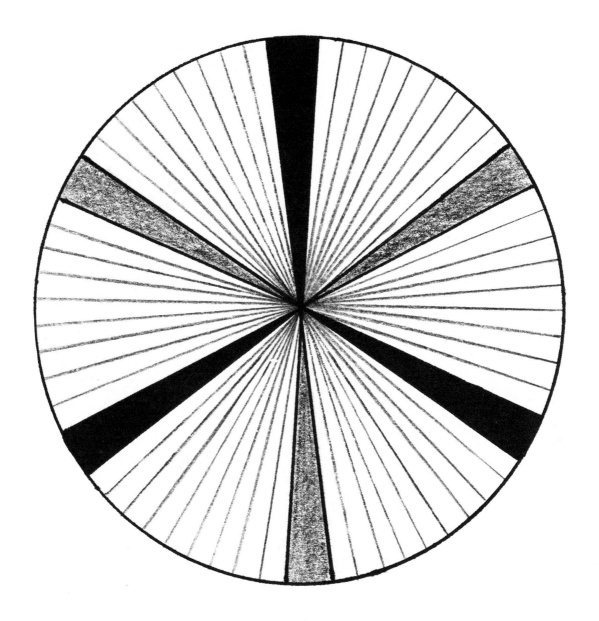

2-15. The 12-point color wheel. The black areas represent primary
colors; the gray, secondary colors; the striped, tertiary colors.

based on the primary colors red, yellow, and blue (colors that cannot be mixed from others) and the secondary colors green, orange, and purple (mixtures of two primaries). Tertiary colors (mixtures of adjacent primary and secondary colors) are placed in between the sections. Although 20th-century color theory has shown that this color wheel is not always accurate, it is a good starting point toward understanding basic color theory.

At the turn of the century an American color theorist, A. H. Munsell, exasperated with the unscientific manner of describing color, decided to divide it into its three properties and to classify all colors by assigning each a scientific number. The three aspects of color are: hue, the name of a color; value, the lightness or darkness of a hue (the addition of white to a hue forms a tint, and the addition of black a shade); and chroma, the brightness or dullness (intensity) of a hue, determined by the addition of its complement. Color can thus be identified by its name, its lightness or darkness, and its brightness or dullness. Munsell assigned numbers to hues based on assessments of their value and intensity. The value scale ranges from darkest (black), #1, to lightest (white), #10. The chroma scale ranges from dull (most gray), #2, to most bright, #14.

In addition to isolating a hue according to its properties Munsell developed his own color wheel based on five primary hues instead of three (figure 2-16). His method of classification has been so successful that it has been adopted by industry. The color relationships on Munsell's color wheel include: principal hues, red, yellow, green, blue, and purple, which are visually equidistant from each other; intermediate hues, which are made by mixing two principal hues together (on the color wheel they are placed between and equally distant from the two component primaries, as red + yellow = reddish yellow [ry]); and complementary hues, which are opposite each other on the color wheel and which, when mixed together, form a neutral color, gray (for example, red and greenish blue). The term "complement" describes the effect of combination on the colors in question: a red placed next to a green appears at its most brilliant and intense and vice versa. The colors enrich, or complement, each other.

Any basic dyer's palette should contain the five principal hues plus black. The best combination that I have found is red, blue, yellow, magenta, cyan (turquoise), and black. By mixing these hues together all secondaries and tertiaries desired can be made. The white yarn and the black dye can create tints and shades, and the complements degrees of intensity.

A word of caution about any color theory. Since it deals with scientific principles that work best under optimum conditions and since all dyestuffs contain small amounts of impurities, what may look perfect in that theory may take some experimentation to

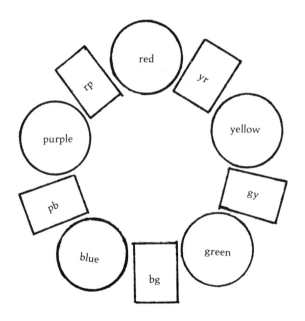

2-16. Munsell's 10-point color wheel. The circles represent principal hues; the rectangles, intermediate hues.

achieve for yourself. With your set of dyes green-blue may not achieve a perfect gray over red: a hue closer to green may work much better. Color theory provides the basic information to start with, but how well you deal with it depends upon your own skills and sensitivity.

The application of color theory to top dyeing demonstrates why it is difficult—in fact, impossible—to achieve a greenish hue over a red area, since they fall on opposite sides of the color wheel, and, when mixed, become grayish brown. Other plans must be made, such as a different dyeing sequence or additional wrapping and unwrapping of certain areas.

Other color combinations are possible as well. Johannes Itten, in his book *The Art of Color* (a reading must for people who deal with color), forms color harmonies through geometric relationships on the 12-point color wheel. Although the 10-point color wheel is much more accurate, the relationships are sound enough to be applied to both. Figure 2-17 illustrates a few of these color harmonies: the split complement (a), which involves a hue and the hues on either side of its complement, and the tetrad (b and c), which denotes two pairs of complements that are used together in the same composition. All the harmonies shown create a neutral color when the component parts are mixed together. This means that all colors of the spectrum are represented in some manner and that harmony is complete.

Color harmonies are primarily the choice of the artist. Everyone has his favorite hues: some prefer the warm side of the spectrum (red, yellow, and orange); others, the cool side (blue, purple, and green); still others, a mixture of the two. Variations of intensity and value will create endless combinations. Observers who prefer the same hues will respond positively to the harmony; those who do not may have trouble feeling comfortable with it.

This consideration of color theory is not designed to present a lot of information but only just enough to help you avoid some of the pitfalls of color mixing and top dyeing. Color theory can and should be explored in greater depth by studying the work of Runge, Goethe, Chevreul, Itten, and Munsell.

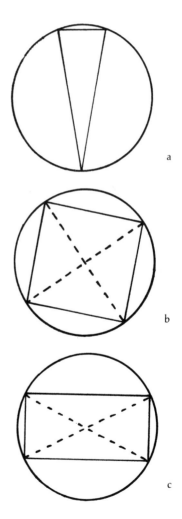

2-17. Some color harmonies from Johannes Itten's *The Art of Color:* (a) split complement, (b) harmonious dyad, (c) harmonious dyad.

Dyeing Techniques

Ikat is a dyeing process: most of the design is determined by the wrapping-and-dyeing procedure. Some fiber artists concentrate on it so heavily that they do very little weaving on an ikat—just a few shots across to hold the yarns in the proper order. Since dyeing plays a large role in ikat technique, it must be mastered in order to obtain the desired results. It is a shame that so many fiber artists do not do their own dyeing but instead rely on commercial colored yarns. Rearranging a design to fit the yarn colors on a sample card or on the studio shelves is shameful. Once I have finished my design, I am ready to begin my project, and waiting for certain colors to be shipped (*if* they are in stock!) would drive me wild. Instead I immediately start dyeing, and I enjoy the break between designing and constructing.

Few fiber artists have the money or the space to stock every hue, with its many varieties of value and intensity. Since it is so hard to anticipate your needs over the next six months or so, it is best to stock a wide assortment of natural-colored yarns and to dye the desired amount as needed. With ikat you have little choice—the design must be dyed into the yarns. Experienced and inexperienced alike must work with color and design in the dyepot.

Before you begin, you should be very familiar with your materials. Before the middle of the 19th century, when synthetic, or coal-tar, dyes became available, there were only vegetable dyes. The materials were familiar local plants, and the dye recipes had been handed down for centuries. The process was well known, and there was little chance of failure. Today there is a wide variety of synthetic dyes on the market, each geared for certain fibers and each with its own procedure.

Any class of dyestuffs will consistently give good results if you have done your homework. That means being familiar with the dyeing process, either the one outlined here or your own version. It also means experimenting with the class of dyes that you choose to use. Do not depend upon the color notations on the dye chart: do your own testing. Wind test samples and dye all the colors ordered so that you have a specific idea of what color turkey red, for example, is. For ikat it also means trying top-dyeing experiments as well so that you do not have to guess or pray about what the final result will look like.

All your samples should be carefully labeled and compiled in a looseleaf notebook much like that shown in figure 3-1. Then you will not need to make

3-1. A dyer's notebook, full of invaluable information about past dyepot results.

new tests for each new project but can instead easily refer to the samples that you made before.

Purchase a set of dyes that contains the five principal hues, for they can be mixed to create almost any color needed. Since dyes are not pure color—only colors in the light spectrum are—all hues cannot be mixed from the three primaries alone. Each dye hue is a mixture of chemicals that together appear to be a certain color. If you have trouble classifying a brand name and want specific information on it, look it up in the *Color Index* (see Appendix B).

If you want to use vegetable dyes with the ikat technique, great! You will be following the beautiful tradition of all ikat. Vegetable dyes are still used exclusively in many cultures, and the processes are highly ritualized. Indigo is the most basic color for traditional ikats, and it would be welcome in contemporary work as well. Justice could not be done in this chapter to the countless recipes for vegetable dyeing. If you are not familiar with this type of dyeing, there are several excellent books on the market that will give you all the information you need (see the Bibliography). Vegetable dyes are used in the same manner as commercial dyes in the ikat process.

DYE CLASSIFICATIONS

There are various classifications of dyes, three of which are the best known and most accessible. Other dye classes are used with fiber techniques, and their instructions can be applied if necessary or desirable. The dyes that are discussed here are: household or all-purpose, direct, and acid. Each has its own particular properties, and all are used with one of the dyeing procedures outlined later in this chapter.

The most common type are household or all-purpose dyes. They are easily obtainable from local stores and are familiar to most people. Household dyes can be used on all animal and plant fibers and on some synthetics. This applicability has both advantages and disadvantages. Because they are manufactured for use on such a wide variety of fibers, they tend to be wasteful. A household dye is in fact a combination of dyestuffs, some for animal fibers, some for plant fibers, and others for synthetics. In dyeing cotton, for example, only particles capable of reacting with cotton are activated, a small percentage of the powder in the envelope. The rest of the particles are poured down the drain and wasted. Because of their all-purpose composition, however, you need only one set of dyes to color all types of fibers. They are great for fibers of unknown composition.

The ability of household dyes to color "everything" also involves a higher percentage of impurities in the hue, which is especially important in top dyeing fibers for ikat. My main irritation lies in the names assigned to the colors. If I ask students to collect the primary hues for samples and they come back with Egyptian red, sky blue, and canary, I do not have an accurate idea of the colors, and the color charts are not accurate. The names may be catchy, but I would appreciate an explanation of the color. Does the green lean to the yellowish side of the spectrum or to the blues? If I'm top dyeing with purple, that is an important question. A notation in terms of Munsell's numerical classification would be great.

Nonetheless, you should not pass these dyes up entirely. Their accessibility makes them worthwhile. To obtain a certain hue—say, red—buy several reds and test them until you have the color you want. A package of dye will generally color a pound of yarn to a medium shade. Darker colors require more dyestuff. Either acetic acid or salt is used as the assistant (to help set the colors), depending on the fiber that is being dyed.

Acid and direct dyes are the other major classes. Each of these is constructed for use on certain fibers. Acid dyes are used for animal (protein) fibers—silk, wool, alpaca, and goathair, among others. Direct dyes are used for plant (cellulose) fibers, such as cotton, linen, and jute. They come in concentrated form and will generally dye up to eight times more fiber than an equal amount by weight of an all-purpose dye. Each type of dye has its own assistant to help ensure colorfastness: acid dyes use acetic acid, and direct dyes salt. Because they are specifically keyed for certain fibers, there is little waste in the dyebath. In fact, you may often find that the dyebath is completely exhausted—with only clear water remaining—a reason to celebrate. These dyes exhibit good wash- and lightfastness.

Although acid and direct dyes are not as easy to obtain, the serious fiber artist should have a set of each on hand. More and more suppliers will sell these dyes to the small buyer. A small order generally means 1 pound or less of each hue needed. To the large distributor this is really small potatoes, for they stock their dyestuffs in 100-pound containers. A person who requests 1-pound quantities is mostly an irritation, yet some will fill your order. A hefty packaging charge is usually included. A pound of this dyestuff goes a long way, and it is a good feeling to know that you have enough dye on hand to do most jobs. Again, once you have your set of dyes, test them thoroughly before embarking on an ikat. It may succeed without testing, but you are taking a chance.

BASIC DYEING PROCEDURE

Dyeing, like any other process, requires careful attention to the procedure over a period of time in order to develop skill. As with any technique, you will make mistakes and your results may be occasionally disappointing, but don't let that discourage you—keep at it. I once made a terrible mistake in dyeing a very large ikat for an important client. Since everything was wrapped but my dyepot was not large enough for the whole piece, I divided it into two halves and used two dyepots at the same time. I was not as careful as I should have been in measuring the dyestuff, and, sure enough, when the piece dried, one side was definitely lighter than the other. I panicked and was sure that I would have to do the whole piece over again. Since I had nothing to lose, I tried to redye the lighter side to obtain the proper intensity. Through sheer force of will and terror I redyed and redyed until the hues matched. What a waste of time and effort because of a stupid mistake! I learned my lesson.

There are two ways to approach the measurements for dyeing. You can measure and weigh carefully, using the most accurate methods and equipment. Or you can make rougher measurements with handy kitchen equipment—teaspoons and cups. Neither is more correct than the other: each requires a certain personality. The scientific dyer would be appalled by the thought of such slipshod methods, and the teaspoon dyer could not be bothered. What is important is that all measurements must be made as accurately as possible with the chosen equipment. This will ensure repeatable and predictable results. No matter whether you choose to use teaspoons and empty jelly jars or sensitive gram scales and calibrated cylinders, it's the results that are important. The directions below can be followed with either approach.

Equipment

Following is a list of the necessary equipment (figure 3-2):

1. large enamel or stainless-steel pot or kettle—never use aluminum (canning pots are great)
2. stirring rods, dowels, wooden spoons, or plexiglass rods
3. small stainless-steel or enamel pan for mixing dye paste
4. glass or plastic teaspoons and cups for measuring or comparable laboratory equipment—graduated cylinders and beakers
5. gram or ounce scale for weighing dyestuff and yarn
6. candy thermometer
7. metal spatula for mashing dyepaste
8. tags and waterproof pen for marking skeins
9. quart jars or laboratory bottles to store dye stock
10. tea strainer lined with cloth

3-2. Some basic equipment for dyeing.

Materials

Following is a list of the necessary materials (figure 3-3):

1. acetic acid for acid dyes—white vinegar may also be used, but it is too expensive for frequent use (glacial acetic acid can be purchased at a photography-supply store)

2. uniodized salt for direct dyes

3. Glauber's salt (sodium sulfate), a leveling agent (optional)

4. set of either direct or acid dyes or packages of household dyes

3-3. Commercial dyestuffs and fixative chemicals.

3-4. A detail of a Sumba, Indonesia warp ikat, with an undyed stripe in the fringe.

Procedure for Direct, Acid, and Household Dyes

1. Have the equipment assembled for ready use.
2. Weigh and skein the yarn. Divide the yarn into ¼-pound or smaller skeins: do not use a 1-pound skein of yarn. Smaller skeins ensure better water circulation, less chance of streaking, and easier movement of the yarn. Tie each skein loosely in several places. Weigh the yarn in ounces or grams and record. Arrange the wrapped ikat carefully in the dyepot so that it is evenly surrounded by the dyebath. The ends do not have to be placed in the dyebath: they can rest on crossed dowel rods. The undyed ends are later cut off or incorporated into the design, as in figure 3-4.

3. Wet out the yarn. Wash the yarn in warm (90°) soapy water and add a water softener if necessary. If the yarn has not been previously dyed, it will contain spinning oil and must be carefully washed and rinsed several times. Let the yarn soak in soapy water in preparation for the dyebath. For really greasy yarn add ammonia or washing soda and rinse well.

4. Measure and place the desired amount of warm water into the dyepot. You can usually count on using 2½ gallons of water per pound of yarn. More water can be added for lighter colors, a little less for darker ones. If you are using less water, the pot must be stirred more often to help prevent streaking.

5. Measure or weigh the dye powder and pour it into the dyebath (figure 3-5). If you are using packaged dyes, empty the desired amount into a small pan or jar. Add a little cold water to the powder and mash it into a smooth paste with the metal spatula. Dissolve the paste with a cup of boiling water. Pour the mixture through the cloth-lined strainer to catch any lumps. An alternate way to prepare the dyestuff is to make a liquid stock. This is a specific amount of dyestuff in a specific amount of water, creating a dye-to-water ratio. It is especially good for acid or direct dyes, since a little powder goes a long way and you may need only minuscule amounts for color mixing. To make a dye stock, in a quart jar or calibrated laboratory jar dissolve 1 ounce or 30 grams of dyestuff in a quart or liter of boiling water. This creates a 3% stock solution, 1:32 or 3:100. Stir the liquid to remove any lumps. This dye-stock mixture can be stored and used when needed. If it should precipitate later, heat it gently in a pot of water until it redissolves. Make sure to label the jar and the lid. When several jars are open and the lids are sprawled about, they can be replaced correctly. This stock solution can be poured into the dyepot. Use either tablespoons or milliliters as measures. About 5 tablespoons of a stock solution will generally dye ½ pound of yarn to a medium shade. More is needed for darker, more intense colors. Add the dye stock directly to the dyebath.

3-5. Measuring the powdered dyestuff.

6. Measure or weigh the assistant—salt or acetic acid, depending on the type of dye—and add half the needed amount to the dyebath. Reserve the other half. The usual amount is 1 teaspoon glacial acetic acid (¼ cup white vinegar) to ½ pound fiber or 1½ tablespoons salt per ½ pound. Glauber's salt may be added as well. It is a leveling agent that helps prevent streaking. It also slows down the uptake of the dye into the fibers. Use 4 tablespoons per pound of fiber.

7. Add the fiber to the dyebath (figure 3-6). The temperature should be approximately the same as the wetting-out water. This is extremely important for the protein fibers: wool will lose its bouncy body and shrink excessively if the temperature changes too quickly. Lift the yarn out of the wetting-out solution and let the excess water drip off. Place the yarn evenly around the dyepot.

8. Heat the dyebath carefully, checking the temperature and stirring a few times. Increase the temperature of the dyebath until it reaches 180° to 190°, just below simmer. This step should take about 25 to 30 minutes. If it takes less, you are using too much heat. Start timing the dyeing at this point. Lift and turn the fiber carefully in the dyepot, watching the temperature.

9. Simmer the dyebath 20 minutes and then add the rest of the assistants. If possible, lift the yarn out of the dyebath, stir in the assistant, and return the yarn to the pot. It is possible to push the yarn to one side of the pot and add the assistant to the open area, but this method does not ensure quick and even spreading of the additives as well as complete removal of the yarn does.

10. Simmer the yarn for another 30 minutes. At this point you may find that the dyebath has exhausted itself and that the water is clear, especially if you are using an acid dyebath. This means less work rinsing the yarn, since there is little excess dye.

11. Remove the fiber, wash, and rinse carefully (figure 3-7). Always wash the dyed fiber with soap and water—it is easier to remove the excess dye this way. Rinse until the water is clear. With wool either let the dyebath cool before rinsing the yarn or place it in a rinse water that is approximately the same temperature as the dyebath and gradually cool it during the rinsing. Be careful not to handle it excessively.

3-6. Placing the wet yarn into the dyepot.

12. Lay the skeins or the ikat between old towels and blot. Hang to dry away from direct heat or sunshine.

13. Cut a piece of the dyed yarn, tag it, and add to your dye notebook. On the tag list the date, the amounts of dyestuff or powder, the weight of the yarn, the amounts of additives used, and any unusual data. If the fiber is of an unusual composition, note that also. This may sound like a lot of information, but with time you will develop your own shorthand.

3-7. Rinsing the dyed ikat.

Additional Tips

1. A quick and easy test of the color of a dyebath or stock solution before adding the fiber can be made by dipping a piece of blotting paper or paper towel into the mixture.

2. Never judge the color by the wet yarn: it will always appear to be darker. If you want to know the approximate color, pull a few strands out of the dyebath and squeeze them a few times between your fingers or paper towels. Most of the water will be removed, and a more accurate color will show.

3. If the yarn is not the intensity or color desired, it is best to finish the entire process and redye later with more of the stock solution or with a different color. This is also true if you want a very light tint of a hue: reduce the amount of dye stock in the bath, not the dyeing time. To ensure proper absorption and fastness, the entire 1½-hour process must be completed. A dyestuff is composed of many different particles, which, like a time capsule, are taken up into the fiber at different intervals. In order to obtain the proper color, enough time must be allowed so that all particles can be absorbed. Dipping a skein of yarn into a dyebath for only a few minutes to obtain a tint will produce a washed-out hue that is not as rich as that given by the entire process. Adding additional stock to the dyebath halfway through the process will also compromise the final results.

DISCHARGE DYEING AND REPAINTING

It is not unusual for the fiber artist to find that certain parts of the ikat would look much better if they were brighter or that the dye has seeped under the bindings where it is important to have a clear area. At this point consider removing the color. To remove some color does not indicate failure, and, if it enriches the design, by all means do it, but do it cautiously.

To strip color from cotton or wool, make a solution of ½ teaspoon sodium hydrosulphite and ½ teaspoon sodium hydroxide (caustic soda or lye). Dissolve the chemicals in 1 cup of water, carefully heat to 160°, and apply where needed. A light gray or brown tinge will probably remain on the yarn. Rinse the area.

In a pinch chlorine bleach may also be used, although you must again be very careful and the results can vary. Mix equal parts of bleach and water and apply where needed with a paintbrush. Let it set for five minutes and rinse thoroughly in a water-and-vinegar bath to stop the action of the bleach.

The opposite of bleaching an unwanted spot is painting in a desired spot with concentrated dye stock. After unwrapping the ikat you may find that a particular color is needed in another area or that an already colored area needs strengthening. This method should not be employed on large areas of yarn: rewrapping and dyeing are more in order.

Heat a small quantity of the stock solution and paint it on the needed areas. Let dry and, with a steam iron and a piece of wet cloth, lightly steam the areas to help set the dye. Never let the steam iron rest on the surface but rather keep moving it a small space above the fabric. Rinse thoroughly.

Figure 3-8 illustrates a possible top-dyeing sequence. Note how the design emerges little by little with each successive dyebath. The richness and depth of hue of the areas exposed to all the dyebaths make the ikat glisten like a jewel.

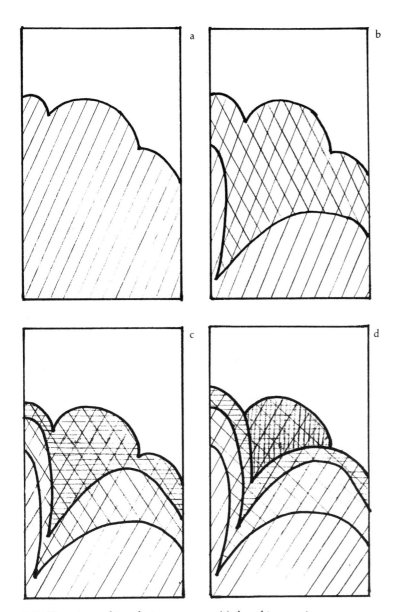

3-8. Wrapping and top-dyeing sequence: (a) the white area is
wrapped, and the unwrapped (striped) dyed yellow; (b) the bottom
of the yellow area is wrapped, and the rest of the fiber dyed
orange; (c) the bottom of the orange area is wrapped, and the fiber
dye red; (d) the bottom of the red area is wrapped, and the
remaining unwrapped fiber dyed in a blue-green dyebath,
which results in a brownish-black hue.

Warp-, Weft-, and Double-ikat Techniques

At this point you may feel that there are just too many things to consider before weaving an ikat and that the technique is too complicated. To those of you who are feeling this way I just want to say, stick with it. Like any technique, it may be hard and time-consuming to walk carefully through it the first few times, but once you learn, the procedure will not require the elaborate preparations described here.

BASIC EQUIPMENT
Following is a list of the basic equipment for warp, weft, and double ikats (figure 4-1):

1. a work table long enough to accommodate the length of the yarn to be wound

2. two 2'-×-4' pieces of wood roughly 1' wider than the *width* of the piece that you intend to weave (for a warp ikat); the *length* of the piece, for a weft or double ikat

3. 3"-long strong nails, hammered every ½" along the width of the boards

4. four large, strong C-clamps to hold the beams to the winding surface

5. strips of plastic, slit garbage bags, or commercial plastic bands (figure 4-2) can be bought for the wrapping

6. two yardsticks or measuring tapes

7. strong, smooth two- or three-ply yarn (fuzzy yarn will stick and make shed changing a real chore), suitable for a warp, carefully measured according to the specifications required by your design, and wound into balls, pull-out skeins, or on tubes to ensure easy and speedy flow during winding

8. strong cord

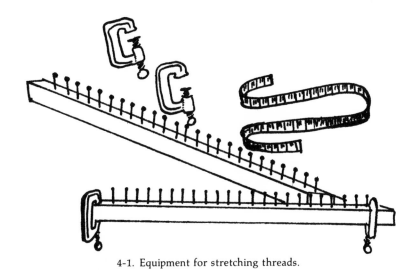

4-1. Equipment for stretching threads.

4-2. Commercial plastic wrap for binding the yarns.

WARP IKAT
Measuring the Yarn
1. Determine the suitable number of warps to the inch for your pattern and for the weave you have chosen. To do this, wind your yarn around a pencil or a dowel rod for 2" or 3". Using the middle portion, measure 1" and count the number of winds. This figure represents the number of warps per inch for a warp-faced weave; half this number is the number of warps per inch for a 50/50 weave.

2. Determine the length of the warp. Allow plenty of room for the ikat pattern. Be sure to include sufficient yarn to allow for: (a) shrinkage during dyeing, (b) takeup during weaving, and (c) the normal amount of loom waste. Estimate too much rather than too little: many an ikat has ended up with the pattern falling off into the fringe.

Winding the Yarn
1. Clamp the wooden beams to the table, carefully measuring both sides to ensure correct position in relation to the length of the warp.

2. Have the yarn ready in pull-out skeins or balls for easy removal in order to maintain even tension while winding (figure 4-3). The yarn should be either white, a natural color, or the first color to be retained and wrapped in the design. This may require dyeing the yarn prior to this winding.

3. Make a slip knot on the end of the warp and slip it over the end nail (figure 4-4).

4. Wind the yarn back and forth around the nails the required number of yarns to the ½" for your piece—for example, if you have planned on 20 ends to the inch, wind out 10 lengths.

5. Secure this yarn around the nails further up to hold the tension.

4-3. Materials assembled for the layout of a warp ikat: plastic bags being cut into strips, cord for twining around the warp, and yarn rolled into a ball for easy removal.

4-4. Winding the warp for the first ½".

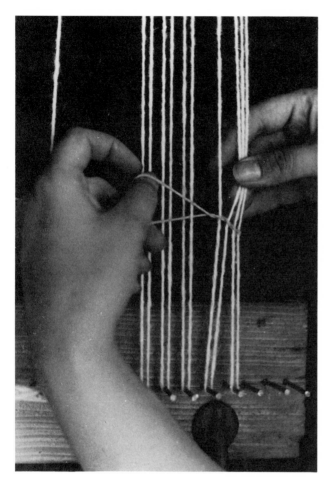

4-5. Twining around individual warp threads to maintain proper sequence at all stages of the process.

4-6. Placing the twined loops on the first nail. Note how the loose end of the warp is wound in a figure eight to maintain warp tension during the twining.

6. Twine cord around each strand of yarn approximately 3″ in from the nails on both ends. Twining is essential, for it serves the function of lease sticks, to keep the proper order of the warp at all times (figure 4-5).

7. After twining both sides slide each loop of yarn one by one onto the first nail (figure 4-6). You have just wound ½″ of the warp. Continue this process until the entire width of the warp is wound (figure

4-7). It is important to do all the winding at one time: if you discontinue warping before it is completed and resume at a later time, you may lose evenness of tension.

8. After all the warp has been wound, twine again between each group of yarns on both sides of the nails. This will make it easier to put the yarn back on the nails after dyeing.

4-7. Winding the warp.

4-8. Placing the cartoon under the warp. Heavy outlines around the shapes make the design easier to see through the warps.

Wrapping the Yarns

1. Place the design next to the warp. If your design is a full-size cartoon, slide it under the warp to serve as a guide while you are wrapping (figure 4-8). If it is on graph paper, place it next to you and measure the sections with a ruler.

2. Pick up approximately ½" of the warp yarns whose color you wish to retain. Wrap a plastic strip tightly around this group, pulling it slightly to stretch it taut. Tie the ends with a half-hitch knot (figure 4-9). Continue this procedure until all the areas that should

be reserved from further dyeing are wrapped securely (figure 4-10).

3. Remove the yarns from the wooden beams by loosening the tension and flipping the beams over. Don't be frightened by what may look like a twisted, impossibly tangled pile of spaghetti (figure 4-11). If you have followed the procedure correctly, the yarns will go back on the nails as easily as they came off, as in figure 4-12, which shows the yarns back on the beams after dyeing. The beams will need adjusting to allow for any shrinkage that may result from dyeing.

4-9. Wrapping the design in ½″ bundles.

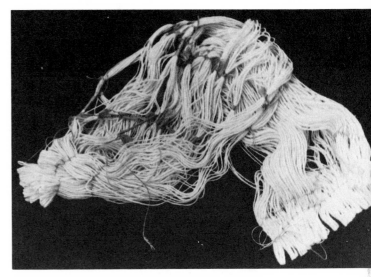

4-11. The warp removed from the beams and ready for the dye-bath.

4-10. Wrapping completed with the first color of the design reserved.

4-12. The dyed warp back on the beams and tied for the second dye-bath.

4-13. Unwrapping the ikat bindings.

Unwrapping the Yarns

After all wrapping and dyeing steps are completed and the yarns are dry, lay the yarns out carefully and unwrap. Be prepared for surprises (figure 4-13). I always feel like I am opening a package. You never really know what has happened under those wrappings. Some of the dyed areas may be disappointing; others will delight you. They may approximate your design very closely or look very different from what you had in mind. The design will again be altered when it is woven: for example, some of the areas may appear very angular after unwrapping, but edges tend to disappear and shapes will develop their characteristically blurred edges with weaving (figure 4-14).

Alternate Warp-ikat Method

For patterns that require little accuracy or detail, such as stripes, it is possible to wind the warp on a conventional warping reel. Make a cross at both ends of the warp and tie loosely with string. Slip each end on a thick dowel rod, spread to the proper width, and tie to the clamped boards. You can then pick out the areas to be wrapped and proceed as usual. This method is not recommended for intricate designs, but it is fast for simple patterns.

4-14. The warp completely unwrapped and ready to place on the loom.

58

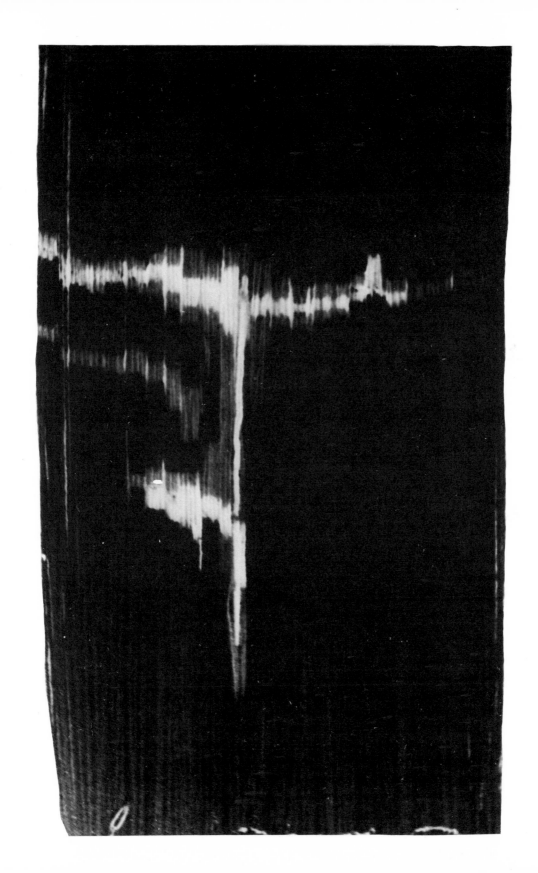

59

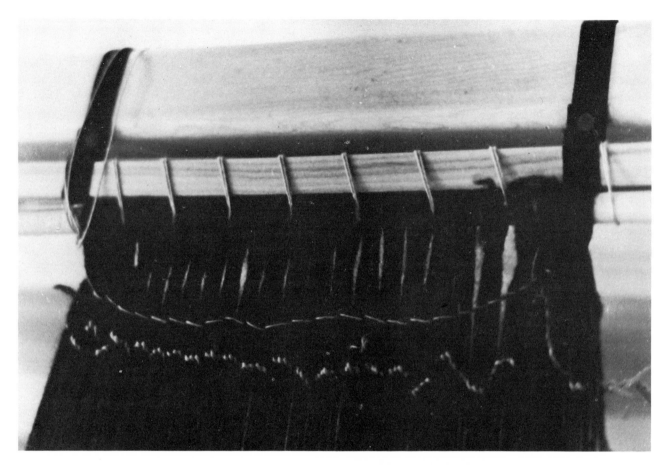

4-15. The warp wrapped around a thick dowel and lashed to the warp beam of the loom.

Weaving

1. Dress the loom with the dyed warp as you would any warp. Some weavers suggest threading from the front of the loom in order to have more control over the design. I always warp from the back and have had no trouble with this method. Your best bet is to use the warping method that you are most accustomed to and not to tackle another new facet in this process. To warp from the back, slip a thick dowel through the looped warp yarns and lash it to the back beam (figure 4-15).

2. In tying the warp pull carefully to maintain the design. If you have used a flexible warp such as wool, you can experiment by pulling some of the threads slightly to alter the pattern. On other warps pulled patterns can be established by tying sections of the warp to the front and back beams in different lengths.

3. Weave a plain weft, especially for a warp-faced weave. Other treadling patterns can be established as well. A weft that is slightly darker or lighter than the background color of the warp will add interest to the areas where it peeks through (figure 4-16).

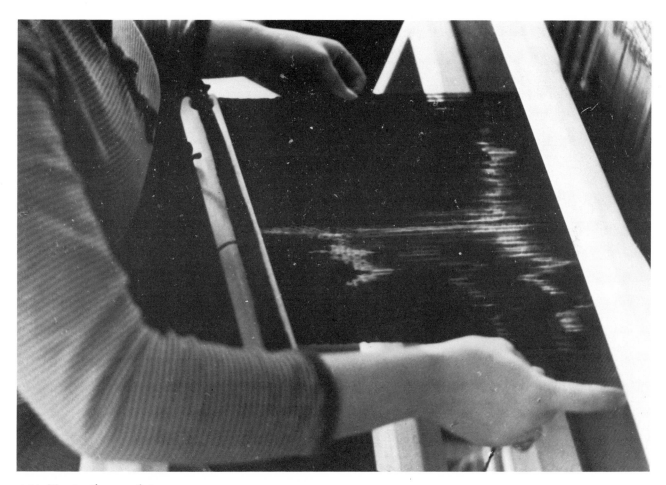

4-16. Weaving the warp ikat.

WEFT IKAT
Equipment

The basic equipment for weft ikat is the same as for warp ikat except that you will also need several shuttles, the number depending upon the size of your piece. With a weft ikat your yarn options are wider. Because the yarns are not placed under tension, a weaker type can be used. A fuzzy or nappy yarn can also be used. Thicker yarns will create coarser designs than thin ones. The texture of your yarns will play an important role in the overall effect of your design.

Measuring the Yarn

1. Determine how many shots will be required per inch. This is extremely important. If your figure is too low, your design will shrink considerably, as if you were viewing it through a concave piece of glass. If your figure is too high, your design will be lengthened and therefore distorted. The only accurate way to determine the correct number of shots per inch is to weave a 3" or 4" sample. For greater accuracy count the shots in the middle portion of your sample. There is always some slippage on the warp of the last few rows of weaving.

2. Determine the length of each shot, allowing room for shrinkage during dyeing, for takeup during weaving, and for the normal amount of loom waste. The measurement must be accurate, or your design will be thrown off.

Winding the Yarn

1. Clamp the wooden beams to the table, measuring both sides to ensure correct position in relation to the width that you have estimated for the weft.

2. Have the yarn ready to be wound so that you can maintain an even tension as you wind.

3. Make a slip knot on one end and place it over the end nail on one side. The number of shots per inch are wound out onto the first and second nails on each end.

4-17. Winding the yarn for a weft ikat.

4. Wind the yarn back and forth around the nails for the required number of inches (figure 4-17).

5. After the entire length has been wound, twine between the ½" groupings on the nails to ensure proper order followed in placing the piece after the dyeing process (figure 4-18). Twining around each length of yarn, as for the warp ikat, is not necessary, since the weft will be wound onto shuttles in the proper order.

4-18. Twining around the ½" bundles to ensure proper replacement of the weft after dyeing.

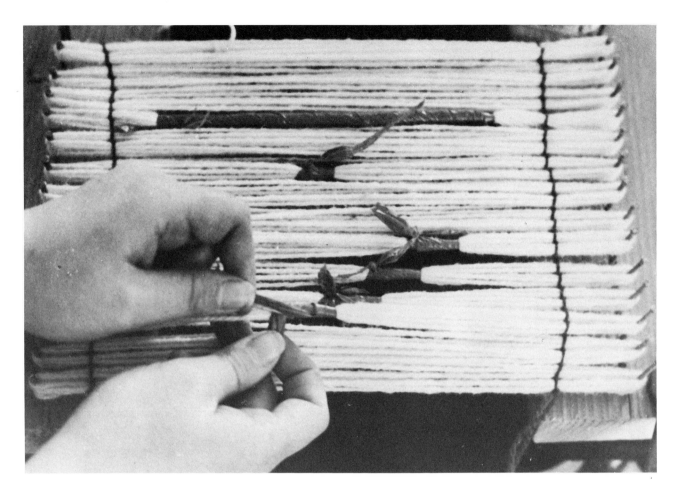

6. Follow the instructions for the warp ikat up to and including the steps for unwrapping. Figure 4-19 shows the wrapping, and figure 4-20, the ikat after dyeing.

7. There are two techniques for proper placement of the pattern after the weft has been wound on shuttles. One, often used on historical ikats, is to wrap and leave undyed a strip down each side of the weft. The spots can be lined up on either end at each shot of the weft during weaving. If a white strip isn't part of your design, replace the unwrapped weft on the nails and run a piece of chalk up and down the ends. These marks will act as guides during the weaving and can be brushed off later.

8. After the weft has been unwrapped, place it back on the nails, untie the twining at the edges, and carefully wind it onto the shuttles, maintaining the winding order. Start from the top of the design and wind

4-20. The weft replaced on the beams after dyeing.

down, labeling the first shuttle (1), the next shuttle (2), and so on. When the piece is ready to be woven, begin with the highest-numbered shuttle and work in reverse order: (1) will be the last shuttle used. Do not be afraid of cutting the yarn at any point when the shuttle is full. There is usually enough play in each row to overlap the beginning or ending yarns.

4-21. The weft wound onto shuttles and woven in a weft-face weave. Notice how the variegated yarn on the shuttle looks as if it would never weave to pattern.

Weaving

1. Insert the first shuttle (with the highest number) and position the dyed areas on the loom. The yarn will sometimes be bent at the edges due to the nails on the beams. This can help serve as a guide for placement.

2. Keep lining up the pattern as you weave. Force your pattern if necessary, or your design will disintegrate. You may have excess yarn at the edges or have to tug slightly to pull it in place.

3. Once you have secured the edges at the proper place on the warp, pull up one large arc in the middle and split it into smaller bubbled sections (figure 4-21). Change your shed and then beat the row down with the beater.

4. If you have estimated too great a length for each weft shot, a few warps can be added to increase the width. If each weft shot is too short, a few warp threads can be left unwoven on one side.

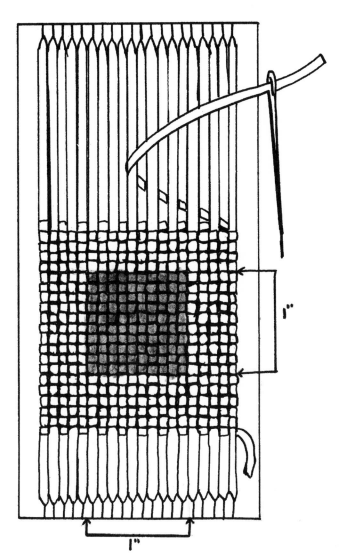

DOUBLE IKAT

For a double ikat it is particularly important to weave a sample first in order to determine the number of warps and wefts per inch. If these counts are not determined accurately, they will wreck your entire pattern. First decide the number of warps per inch: this will determine the number of weft shots. *Do not guess:* just because you are planning a 50/50 weave with 12 warp ends per inch, you may not automatically weave 12 weft shots in the same inch. There can be more or less, and just one off in every inch could ruin your pattern. Every inch off multiplies your problems with correct placement on the warp pattern.

Set up a cardboard loom, as shown in figure 4-22. Warp it for 3″ or 4″ with the proper number of warps per inch. Weave the weft for 3″ or 4″ in the pattern to be used (tabby, twill, basket, etc.). Take a reading of the number of weft shots in the middle and use this calculation in your figuring.

Equipment

The equipment is the same as for the warp and weft ikats, but you will also need a sheet of graph paper for recording.

4-22. The exact number of warps and wefts to the inch can be easily determined by setting up a sample on a simple cardboard loom.

4-23. The weft yarns set up and wrapped for a double ikat, with the cartoon showing through underneath.

Winding the Yarns

For a warp-and-weft, or double, ikat the procedures for winding and wrapping the yarns are the same as for the warp and weft ikat, respectively. Wrap the warp and weft separately, however, using the same cartoon as a guide for each. For the double ikat a full-size cartoon of the design is best: placing the same drawing under both the warp and the weft as they are being wrapped separately maintains the minimum amount of deviation from the pattern.

Figures 4-23 and 4-24 show the steps for the weft, which is wrapped, dyed, and shown with the cartoon underneath partially removed. The warp of the ikat is shown in figure 4-25 with the same cartoon beneath it, and in figure 4-26 with the cartoon removed.

Dye the warp and the weft in the same dyepot if possible to ensure the same color. If there is too much yarn to fit easily in the dyepot, make careful calculations of the dyeing process so that the color can be duplicated as closely as possible.

4-24. Wrapped warp yarns for the same double ikat, after dyeing and with the cartoon partially removed.

4-25. Warp threads with the design completely wrapped, showing the cartoon underneath.

Marking the Pattern

After unwrapping the warp and the weft lay out the yarns. Stretch the weft on the frame and carefully place the warp next to it. Have the patterns facing you in the way in which you want them to be woven— either the back or the front of the weaving will be facing you, depending on how you plan to weave it. Make the following notations on the graph paper and on the warp and the weft.

1. Mark the lower right-hand corner and upper right-hand corner of the warp. Use a black marking pen, chalk, or pieces of yarn. This will help you to warp the loom correctly, as you will match these notations with the right-hand side of the loom.

2. Roughly sketch the design of the ikat on the graph paper (in reverse if you are weaving it with the back side toward you) and note the following on the graph paper.

  a. How many inches of background or border are to be woven before the ikat design is reached? This can also be marked in chalk on the warp.

  b. From what side does the last piece of weft to be wound on to a shuttle come? Mark the correct side on the graph paper. This will prevent you from beginning the weft shot from the wrong side and having your weft pattern go in the opposite direction from the warp pattern.

  c. On each side of the weft, as before, run a piece of colored chalk up and down the ends, marking the beginning and end of each shot.

4-26. The same warp threads as in figure 4-25 but with the cartoon completely removed.

Weaving

The same rules apply as for warp and weft ikats. Remove the yarn (figure 4-27) and number the shuttles, as for the weft ikat. Weave in a normal manner (figure 4-28). Keep lining up the pattern as you weave. Do not let it wander for even one shot. If you have extra weft at some point, pull a small loop to the back of the weaving. Such loops can later be cut and threaded into the weave (figure 4-29).

A double ikat is doubly exciting to weave, because you are controlling two patterns simultaneously. When one border matches another or two tiny dots line up perfectly, it is a time to rejoice and to be proud of having achieved a perfect match of patterns. A double ikat has even more room for an ambiguous design, since the blurring of the edges is even more pronounced when it occurs in both directions.

4-27. Winding the weft for the double ikat into shuttles.

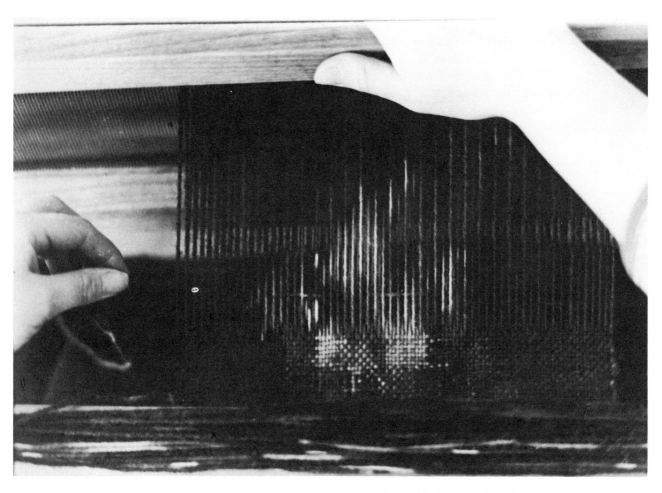

4-28. The double ikat warped on the loom, with the weft being pushed into place for a 50/50 weave.

4-29. Loops pulled to help maintain the pattern. They can be located either in the middle and left on the back of the weaving or twisted at the edges and reinserted at the back into the selvages.

ISOLATING DESIGN AREAS

If you want to try a subtractive approach to ikat design or if it is necessary to unwrap certain areas of a design before the final dyebath, specific wrappings must be isolated in some manner.

A subtractive approach to ikat means that the entire design is wrapped on the white yarns and that the areas to be dyed are unwrapped with each successive dyebath. On the last dyebath you are left with bindings only on these parts that are to remain white.

It is sometimes also necessary to unwrap certain areas of a design before completing the binding process. For example, if you are using complementary hues in the same design, in order to achieve the second hue after dyeing the first—say, a purple after a yellow—the yarns must remain white during the yellow dyebath and later, after the yellow area has been wrapped, the areas to be purple must be unwrapped and dyed.

To isolate areas to be unwrapped later, several methods can be employed. One is to wrap those areas in another color of plastic. There are various colors of garbage bags on the market, or you can use balloons for wrapping. It is easy to determine later which are to be removed. The second method, used on the island of Rote, is a system of knots. All the knots for the bindings are tied with one knot for the first dyebath, two knots for the second, and so on. Areas that need to be removed later can be identified by the type of knot securing the bindings.

Contemporary Ikat

Many contemporary fiber artists have discovered ikat and are using its characteristics in their work. As they are not bound by a rigid tradition, they are free to explore ikat effects in a variety of ways, some of which are described and illustrated here.

One type of contemporary ikat is a modern interpretation of traditional forms such as the strip-warp ikat used by a variety of cultures. Joanne Segal Brandford combines two different patterns of strip ikat in *American Legion* (figures 5-1 and 5-2), alternating two patterns of warp strips on the loom and then weaving the whole piece at once. An additional element, two types of yarn, one thin and tightly spun and the other thick and soft, accentuates the rippling effect and the differences of the warp-ikat patterns. Lillian Elliott also combines different warp-ikat strips to create a light, lyrical feeling in *Light Show* (figure C-5). The strips and the touch of blue within the piece are arranged in an asymmetrical way not often seen in

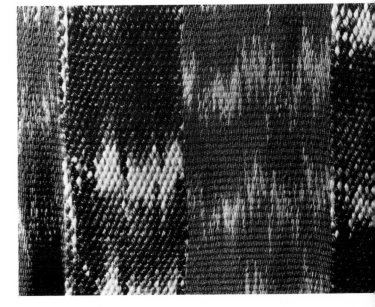

5-2. Joanne Segal Brandford, *American Legion* (detail). Photo courtesy of Hillel Burger.

5-1. Joanne Segal Brandford, *American Legion*, 1970. Linen, vat-dyed, warp-faced plain weave with plaited fringes (top and bottom), warp ikat, 21″ × 45″. Photo courtesy of Hillel Burger.

strip ikats. A traditional technique was employed to create the feeling of shadows and spotlights in light-show happenings during the psychedelic craze.

Warp-ikat yarns pulled into various patterns on the loom are another example of a contemporary use of historical methods. A classic use of the traditional arrowhead effect is shown in Nancy Koprock's shawl (figure 5-3), in which the warp stripes are pulled to form a single point and then woven on a floor loom. Another strong example of the arrowhead effect appears in *Ikat Ribbon Casement* (figure 5-4) by Susan Goldin. This piece was inspired by a collection of old silk ikat ribbons. The warp-ikat strips are pulled into a variety of pointed shapes and spaced on the loom so that the weft filler contains openings and folds that allow light to filter through. The same artist formed a softer, curved pattern with the pulled warp in *Ikat Scroll* (figure 5-5). Its long, thin, vertical format resembles a calligraphic scroll and emphasizes the repeats. An erratic weft of unspun tussah silk is top-laid-in in a thick-and-thin manner in relation to the ikat pattern.

Weft-ikat effects are also used today. Lillian Elliott creates an optical effect in *Whisper* (figure 5-6) by dissolving the diamond shape into the web of a patterned weaving. The diamond form rises from an indefinite image to a strongly contrasted shape, creating a feeling of ascension. A closeup (figure 5-7) of a soft, nubby scarf woven by the same artist shows a complex intertwining line in the weave of the weft ikat.

5-3. Nancy Koprock, shawl, 1975. Bouclé and plied cotton, Cushing dyes, 13¾″ × 109″. The stripes in the warp ikat were pulled to create the arrowhead effect. Photo courtesy of the artist.

5-4. Susan Goldin, *Ikat Ribbon Casement.* Tussah silk, synthetic dyes, 36″ × 60″. The warp-ikat stripes were pulled to create different arrowheads. Photo courtesy of the artist.

5-5. Susan Goldin, *Ikat Scroll*, 1976. Two-ply silk top, synthetic dye, 14″ × 96″. The warp-ikat stripes were pulled into a pattern with an erratic weft. Photo courtesy of the artist.

Double-ikat technique, practiced by few cultures in the past, has a place in contemporary work as well. *Fragment Series II* (figure 5-8) by Joanne Segal Brandford is a double ikat in which the warp and weft are arranged to create a softly checkered effect. The piece is turned 90° so that the warp falls down. Another example of contemporary double ikat (figure C-6) was created by Lillian Elliott. The warp and weft are not matched to one image but rather woven in such a way as to create delicate light and dark areas within the piece. The confusion of the ikat warp and weft is organized by aligning it into plaid arrangement.

5-6. Lillian Elliott, *Whisper*. Silk, wool, and gold thread, weft ikat, 10½″ × 48″. Photo courtesy of Stone and Steccati.

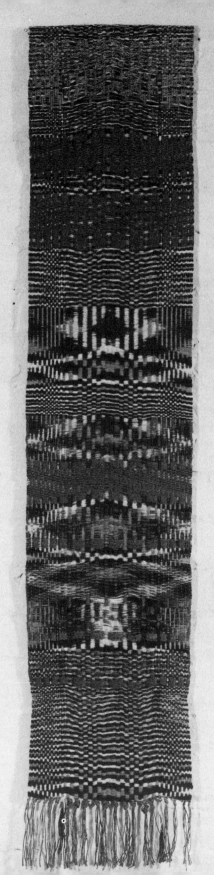

5-7. Lillian Elliott, scarf (detail). Wool, weft ikat. Photo courtesy of the artist.

5-8. Joanne Segal Brandford, *Fragment Series II*, 1973. Linen, vat dyed, double ikat, balanced plain weave with supplementary discontinuous wefts and twining at the warp edges, 55″ × 35″. Photo courtesy of Hillel Burger.

C-1. Sumba, Indonesia, 19th century. Warp ikat, cotton. Collection of Michael Bogle.

C-2. Noto Peninsula, Japan, 1930. Warp ikat, cotton. Photo courtesy of Julie Bagish.

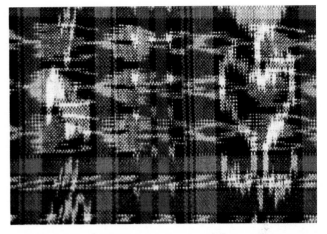

C-3. Guatemala, contemporary. Compound ikat.

C-4. Pana, Guatemala. Weaver working with a warp containing ikat strips.

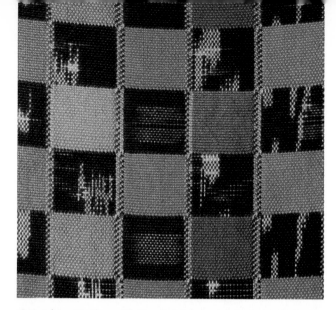

C-5. Lillian Elliott, *Light Show*. Silk, warp-ikat strips woven together, 39″ × 50″. Photo courtesy of Stone and Steccati.

C-6. Lillian Elliott, untitled. Silk, double ikat, 36″ × 42″. Photo courtesy of Stone and Steccati.

C-7. Ichiro Kurihara, *Blocking Ikat*, fabric sample, 1976. Eight-harness block weave, warp and weft ikat, 60 epi (ends per inch) per layer, 10/2 cotton, 7″ × 9″ wide. Photo courtesy of the artist.

C-8. Sarah Haskell, *Come In*, 1974. Wool, rayon, cotton, linen, and wooden door frame; painted warp, woven in six-shaft brocade weave, 30″ × 78″. Photo courtesy of the artist.

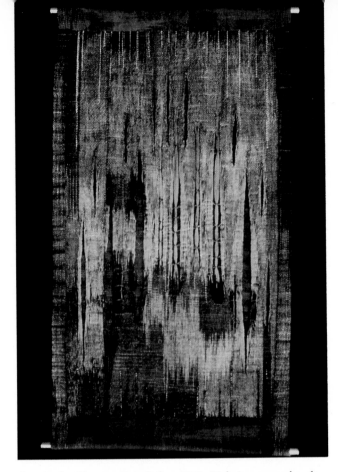

C-9. Lesley Shearer, *Sharon's Piece*, 1973. Mohair warp and weft ikats woven in triple cloth with some slits and leno in plainwoven center, separately woven frame, 3′ × 5′. Photo courtesy of the artist.

C-10. Lesley Shearer, *Audience*, 1976. Mohair over twisted carpet warp, space-dyed yarns woven in separate units with experimental multiple-harness technique, 17″ × 23″ × 3″. Photo courtesy of the artist.

C-11. Bette Mankowski, *Apollo*, 1976. Rayon, warp ikat woven into a cloak. Photo courtesy of the artist.

C-12. Jackie Battenfield, *Colombia I*, 1974. Wool, vat dyed, warp ikat with wrapped warp edges, 36″ × 43″.

C-15. Kristi Kolln, *Folded Pillar*, 1976. Weft ikat woven into long bands and folded together, 18′ tall. Photo courtesy of the artist.

C-16. Susan Goldin, *Knot*. Wool with polyester fiberfill; pulled warp ikat used in tubular weave, stuffed, and manipulated; 10″ diameter × 180″. Photo courtesy of the artist.

C-13. Nancy Koprock. *Breastplate*, 1976. Rayon bouclé and single-ply yarn, vat dyed, 35″ × 100″. Photo courtesy of the artist.

C-14. Sheila Fox, *Transformation*, 1976. Warp ikat (detail) turned 90° and mounted over a frame to create folds, 44″ × 60″. Photo courtesy of the artist.

Incorporating multiple-harness-weaving techniques into ikat is another contemporary approach. A good example of balance between the ikat pattern and the weaving technique is shown in a rug (figure 5-9) by Nancy Sharples. Using a Krokbragd rug technique, the color changes in each weft-ikat shot create blocks within the pattern. The ikat effect is thus blended into the work in a subtle way, and the repeating pattern of the weaving technique is slightly diminished.

Ichiro Kurihara combines an eight-harness block weave with warp and weft ikats in a piece of fabric (figure C-7). The effect is of strongly hued boxes intermixed with the lower value of the ikats, thus containing the movement of the ikat images. Another form controlled by the multiple-harness technique is *Come In* (figure C-8) by Sarah Haskell. Inspired by the springtime landscapes of New England, it combines a very soft ikat design with a brocade pattern. The ikat

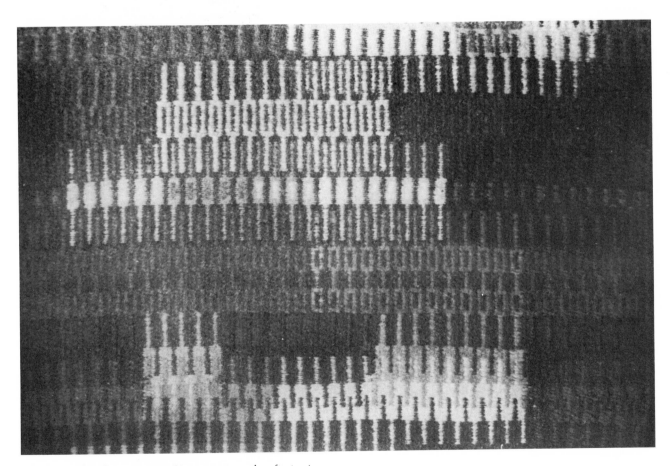

5-9. Nancy Sharples, rug, 1976. Linen warp, wool weft, 4 epi, Krokhragd technique with weft ikat, 40½" × 50". Photo courtesy of the artist.

effect was obtained by painting the yarns with dye and weaving two separate panels that were then set into a wooden door frame, creating the feeling of looking at a foggy landscape through a screen door.

Lesley Shearer works exclusively with complex multiple-harness techniques and often combines them with ikat warps. In *Sharon's Piece* (figure C-9) different ikat warps are used in a triple-cloth technique and enhanced with slits, leno effects, and weft-ikat yarns to expose the colors underneath. Another example of the use of multiple-harness techniques is the double weave shown in *Long Red and Black* (figure 5-10) by the same artist. A red warp ikat is left unwoven and picked up in long floats, complementing the ikat pattern, around the black woven warp, which is brought forward to create the dominant V shapes. The strong forms created by the black warp are softened by the change in value of the red ikat. In *Audience* (figure C-10) the artist creates a three-dimensional work through experimental manipulation of the harness. Color changes in the space-dyed yarns move through the different segments to create an individuality within each unit.

Double weave is used by Dick Sauer in *London Ikat* (figure 5-11) to manipulate the ikat image. The naturally fluid movement of the ikat is contained and released within the vertical stripes that are controlled by the double weave. It makes the few horizontal stripes seem to shoot across the web of this tiny piece.

Clothing can be combined with ikat effects as well. Not just a fabric but an entire cloak can be given a striking ikat design. Figure C-11 shows *Apollo*, a clothing environment by Bette Mankowski. A rainbow of pastel colors makes up the ikat warp of the cloak. The colors are continued with coiling in the headdress and sandals.

5-10. Lesley Shearer, *Long Red and Black*. Double weave, ikat warp left unwoven in long floats, 18″ × 72″. The back and front form mirror images. Photo courtesy of the artist.

Ikat can also be used to produce a strong graphic image almost like painting on a canvas. This is my concept of ikat in *Colombia I* (figure C-12), in which a single complete image is dyed into the fiber and then woven. This piece takes advantage of subtle color changes formed by the seepage of the dye under the bindings, enriching the image. Nancy Koprock also creates a strong design in *Breastplate* (figure C-13), which was inspired by Indian warriors' quill breastplates. Woven on a floor loom without a reed, the colored stripes fall sharply, as if by the effect of gravity, into the center vertical bands.

A minimalist image is represented by Adela Akers in *A Walk By The Shore With Charles* (figure 5-12). The artist states that "large-scale yarn calls for a very large-scale image which reads almost like a closeup, an enlarged detail of a larger image. Bold diagonals, strong shadows—I am concerned in how the part relates to the whole. The haziness of the ikat edge emphasizes the feeling of light and shadow, like long winter shadows on a boardwalk." The effect of the diagonals created by the weft ikat (turned 90°) at that size is striking.

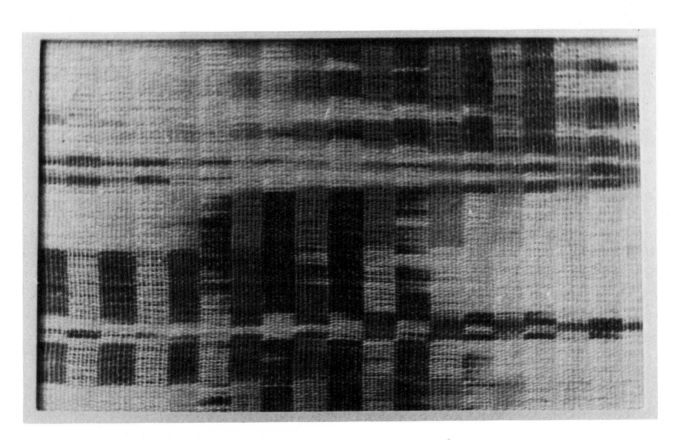

5-11. Dick Sauer, *London Ikat*, 1975. Linen, warp ikat, double weave, turned 90°, one of 30 variations, 4½" × 7½".

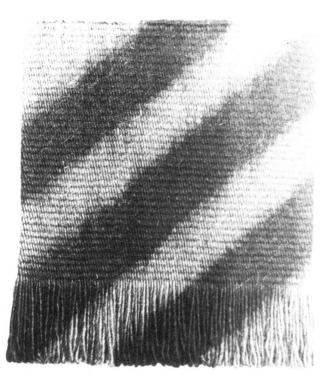

5-12. Adela Akers, *A walk by the shore with Charles*. Heavy one-ply jute and linen, weft ikat, turned 90°, 70″ × 60″. Photo courtesy of the artist.

Sheila Fox concentrates upon the image in her work as well. In *Crescendo* (figure 5-13) the image is accomplished by a gradual change in the width of the horizontal stripes, which rise upward with increasing intensity. In *Transformation* (figures 5-14 and C-14) the ikat is placed over a superstructure that creates folds and ripples, enhancing the color and design changes. In *Converging* (figure 5-15) a shaded diagonal form with a double-ikat effect is created by bands of warps ikats woven together. One band is partially pulled out of line to accentuate the movement.

5-13. Sheila Fox, *Crescendo*. Warp ikat, 32″ × 78″. Photo courtesy of the artist.

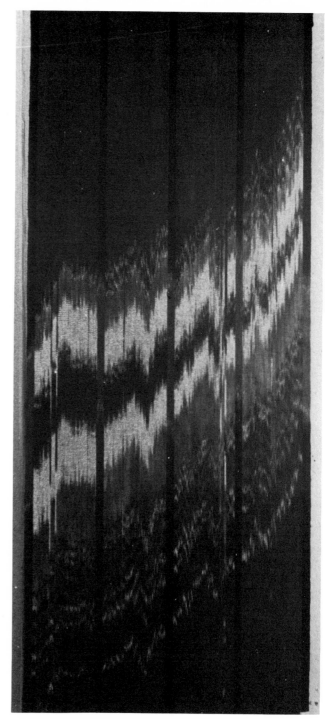

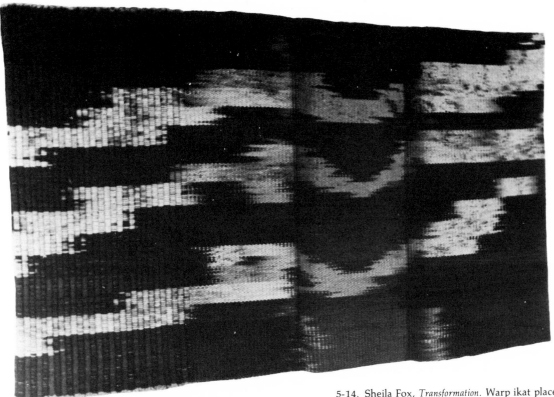

5-14. Sheila Fox, *Transformation*. Warp ikat placed over superstructure to create folds and turned 90°, 44″ × 60″. Photo courtesy of the artist.

5-15. Sheila Fox, *Converging*. Warp-ikat bands woven together to create a double-ikat effect. Photo courtesy of the artist.

Sculptural effects are also applicable to ikat fibers. In *Folded Pillar* (figure C-15) Kristi Kolln uses weft- and warp-ikat yarns to create striped arrangements of color in long woven bands that are later folded together to show the effects of gravity pulling them apart. The concept was to make a simple, childish paper technique monumental. Susan Goldin wove a long tubular shape from a pulled warp ikat and stuffed it to construct *Knot* (figure C-16). The result is a woven form that can be manipulated—reshaped to suit a mood—and either hung or left freestanding. *Ikat Melting Cloth* (figure 5-16) by Lesley Shearer is another example of the combination of ikat with more sculptural forms created by a triple weave on a weighted warp. Additional effects are obtained with wrapping and soumak.

There are other ways of achieving ikat effects. Warp painting is one method. The loom is dressed from the front, through the reed and the heddles, and the warp is carefully laid out in proper order on a long plastic-covered board attached to the front of the loom (figure 5-17). Concentrated dye is painted directly onto the warp and allowed to dry, and the piece is woven as desired (figure 5-18). This method is good for complex designs that call for extreme wrapping procedures or for color combinations that are hard to arrange with top dyeing. It does not produce the depth of hue that vat dyeing does, but that may not be necessary to your design.

For large colored areas, subtle value changes in hue, or stripes you can skip the wrapping and simply dip parts of the warp or weft into the dyepot. That is how the color change was arranged in *Audience* (figure C-10) by Lesley Shearer. Another method, used by Sheila Fox in *Converging* (figure 5-15), is to attach a stencil to the warp or weft yarns and then to spray the dye directly on the fibers.

Ikat has only begun to be explored by contemporary fiber artists. All fiber techniques can be combined with ikat to create new effects or even to emphasize old ones. Whether your particular interest is in fibers, yardage, wall hangings, or freestanding sculpture, ikat effects can be incorporated into your designs. The excitement generated by manipulating the changing colored yarns is well worth exploring.

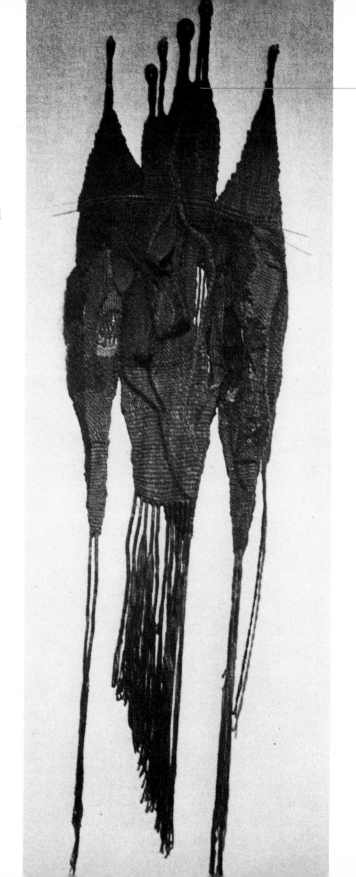

5-16. Lesley Shearer, *Ikat Melting Cloth.* Wool, warp ikat woven with weighted warp under different tensions, with wrapping and soumak, 21″ × 56″. Photo courtesy of the artist.

90

5-17. A warp to be painted is placed in proper order on the board in front of the loom.

5-18. The warp with the painted design completed, ready to be wound on the warp beam.

Appendix A. Watercolor Technique for Designing Ikats

The best way to duplicate some of the effects of ikat on fiber is to design with watercolors on paper. Ikat depends a great deal on the dyebath, and watercolors simulate its properties. They run and blur at the edges when they are used in a watery state, which again makes them compatible with ikat. Watercolors are especially suited to an ikat style that relies heavily on top-dyeing effects. With this technique anticipating what will happen makes the difference between achieving dull colors and bright ones. The steps are described and illustrated below.

1. Place a sheet of heavy watercolor paper on a flat surface that can remain undisturbed until the watercolor dries. A piece of heavy Masonite is good, and it can be moved about if the table surface beneath it is needed. Secure all the edges with brown paper tape or drafting tape.

2. Dampen the paper thoroughly with clean water and a clean brush (figure A-1). Watch for buckling: if it occurs, lift up the tape, stretch the paper slightly, and reseal.

3. Make up a large amount of each color that you are planning to use. The best watercolors come in tubes. The pigment is already in a liquid state, and it is easy to mix large quantities of the wash. An alternative is to use the actual dyes planned for the piece. Mix up a smooth, concentrated solution. This will give you an accurate color notation. Mix the pigments either on a large watercolor palette or in another container. Styrofoam meat trays are good.

4. Lay down the first color, which should be what you plan to use as your first dyebath. Any white areas in the design should not be painted. These are the areas that would be wrapped first in your ikat. Any areas that you plan to unwrap in the middle of the ikat process should also remain white and should be painted later. The remainder of the paper should be saturated with the first color (figure A-2).

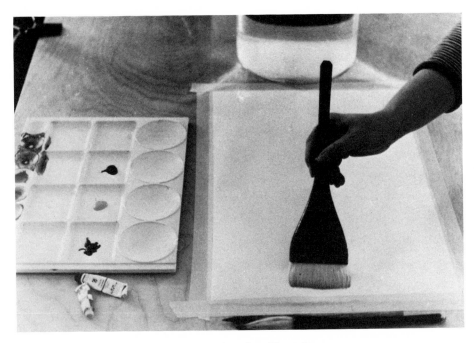

A-1. Moistening the watercolor paper taped to the table surface.

A-2. Applying the first color wash to the paper.

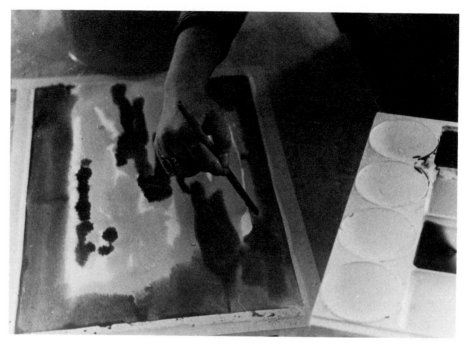

A-3. The second wash applied, reserving areas of the first color.

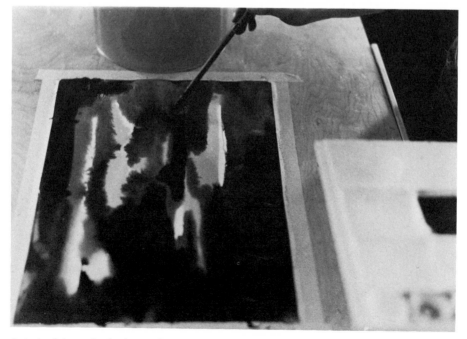

A-4. Applying a third color wash.

A-5. The completed design. All washes have blended together in overpainted areas, as they would in top dyeing.

5. Lay down the second color before the first one dries. Do not paint any areas that are to remain either white or the first color (figure A-3). Where the first and second colors meet, they mix, forming a new color. This is much like what happens in the dyepot during top dyeing.

6. Continue to lay down each successive color that you plan to use in your ikat (figure A-4).

7. The final result can be analyzed in terms of color mixing, complexity of wrapping, and design elements (figure A-5).

I find this method a good tool for designing ikats. Since I often work with a single graphic image, I can tape eight or nine sheets of watercolor paper at a time and work on them all at once. Good ideas can emerge and be refined later. Or the reverse process can be used: an already designed image can be painted to anticipate the ikat effects.

Appendix B.
The Color Index

In ordering commercial dyes or identifying those that you already own, you will notice that each has a proper name, which often relates to the company that manufactures it. This name is usually followed by a descriptive phrase that supposedly alludes to the color therein, but this color often has no basis in reality. The industry standard for identifying dyestuffs, colorfastness ratings, and application is the *Color Index* (CI), published jointly by the American Association of Textile Chemists and Colorists and the Society of Dyers and Colorists in Great Britain. It can be found in most large libraries. This publication will aid you in identifying the true color of a commercial dyestuff as well as its applications and fastness ratings. (It does not carry descriptions of household, or all-purpose, dyes.)

Following are some tips on how to use the *Color Index*.

1. Record the proper name of the dyestuff along with all the information available on the label, including the manufacturer's name.

2. Locate your commercial name in volume IV. A page reference will be given to part I. Turn to the volume that contains part I and locate your dyestuff. Both volume IV and part I will contain the CI number.

3. In part I you will find the following information on your dyestuff: applications (for dyeing and printing), fastness properties on various fibers, hue description (often different from the manufacturer's), textile usage, and nontextile usage.

The *Color Index* will give you the specific information that you may need before ordering a set of dyes. It can help you choose between two closely matched hues or supply applications for top dyeing.

Bibliography

Bird, Junius, "A Pre-Spanish Peruvian Ikat." *Bulletin of the Needle and Bobbin Club*, 1947, 31 (1 & 2), pp. 72–77.

Boyd, E., "Ikat Dyeing in Southwestern Textiles." *El Palacio*, vol. 68, #3, autumn 1961, pp. 185–189.

Bühler, Alfred, "Dyes and Dyeing Methods for Ikat Threads." *Ciba Review*, 1942, #44, pp. 1597–1603.

———, "Ikating in Europe." *Ciba Review*, 1942, #44, pp. 1621–1622.

———, "The Ikat Technique." *Ciba Review*, 1942, #44, 1586–1596.

———, "The Origin and Extent of the Ikat Technique." *Ciba Review*, 1942, #44, pp. 1604–1611.

Burnham, Harold B. and Dorothy K., *Early Hand-Weaving in Eastern Canada*. University of Toronto Press, 1972, pp. 90–93.

Harcourt, Raoul d', *Textiles of Ancient Peru and their Techniques*. Edited by Grace G. Denny and Carolyn M. Osborne. Seattle, University of Washington Press, 1962, pp. 68–70.

Held, Shirley E., *Weaving: A Handbook for Fiber Craftsmen*. New York, Holt, Reinhart, and Winston, 1973, pp. 290–296.

Ikle, Charles F., "Ikat Technique and Dutch East Indian Ikats." *Bulletin of the Needle and Bobbin Club*, 1931, 15 (1 & 2), pp. 2–59.

Itten, Johannes, *The Art of Color*. Translated by Ernst van Haagen. New York, Van Nostrand Reinhold Company, 1961.

Larsen, Jack Lenor with Bühler, Alfred and Solyon, Garrett and Bronwen, *The Dyer's Art: Ikat, Batik, Plangi*. New York, Van Nostrand Reinhold Company, 1976.

Mueller, Conrad G. and Rudolph, Mae, *Light and Vision*. New York, Life Science Library, Time, Inc., 1966.

Munsell, A. H., *A Color Notation*. Munsell Color, 1946.

Ritch, Diane and Wada, Yoshiko, *Ikat: An Introduction to Japanese Ikat, Warp, Weft, Figure*. Kasuri Dyeworks (copyright).

Rushfelt, Joy, "Revival of Ikat Offers Many Possibilities of Experiment." *Handweaver and Craftsman*, vol. 19, #2, Spring 1968, pp. 14–17.

Schera, Cynthia, "Notes on Ikat." *Handweaver and Craftsman*, vol. 24, #2, March–April 1973, pp. 6–8.

Steinmann, Alfred, "The Patterning of Ikats." *Ciba Review*, 1942, #44, pp. 1612–1618.

Tidball, Harriet, *Color and Dyeing*. Shuttle Craft Monograph Sixteen, 1965.

Van Stan, Ina, "A Peruvian Ikat from Pachacamac." *American Antiquity*, 1957, 23 (2), pp. 150–159.

Suppliers

Aljo Dyes
116 Prince Street
New York, New York 10012
direct and acid dyes

Estelle Post Batiks & Imports
4980 Dundas Street West
Islington, Ontario
Canada M9A 1B7
ESPO cold-water dyes, batik supplies

Fezandie and Sperrle, Inc.
111 8th Avenue
New York, New York, 10013
direct and acid dyes

Kasuri Dyeworks
P.O. Box 7101
Berkeley, California 94704
plastic tape for wrapping

Keystone Aniline & Chemical Co., Inc.
321 North Loomis Street
Chicago, Illinois 60607
Keco acid dyes

Straw Into Gold
P.O. Box 2904
Oakland, California 94618
CIBA dye sets, plastic tape for wrapping

Index

looms 12, 20, 52, 58, 60, 62, 66, 67, 70, 72, 75, 76, 87, 90, 91

netting *see* knotted netting

pattern *see* design
    stick 22
plain weave *see* weaves, plain
plaiting 32
plangi 11, 12
pulling 20, 21, 60, 76, 78, 84, 88, 89

repainting 48–49
resist *see* dyeing, resist

selvage 73
shade 36
silk 12, 20, 21, 22, 32, 40, 76, 78, 82
soumak, 89, 90
stripes *see* design, stripe
strips *see* bands

tabby weave *see* weaves, tabby
tapestry *see* weaves, tapestry

tie-dyeing *see* dyeing, tie-
tint 36, 48
top dyeing *see* dyeing, top
twill weave *see* weaves, twill
twining 54, 63, 64, 80
tying 15, 20

value 36, 37, 38, 90

warp 12, 15, 20, 21, 22, 23, 24, 32, 33, 50, 52, 53, 54, 55, 56, 57, 58, 60, 62, 66, 67, 68, 69, 70, 72, 76, 78, 80, 81, 83, 85, 86, 89, 90, 91
    painting 90, 91
weaves
    basket 67
    brocade 82, 85
    double 32, 86, 87
    50/50 13, 31, 33, 52, 67, 72
    gauze 22
    leno 32, 83, 86
    multiple-harness 82, 83, 85, 86
    plain 60, 75, 80, 83
    tabby 32, 67

tubular 84
twill 32, 33, 67
warp-faced 12, 13, 32, 33, 52, 60, 75
weft-faced 32, 66
weaving 9, 11, 16, 22, 24, 32, 38, 50, 52, 58, 60, 62, 64, 65, 66, 67, 70, 73, 75, 76, 78, 82, 83, 85, 86, 87, 38, 89, 90
weft 12, 20, 21, 22, 23, 24, 32, 33, 60, 62, 63, 64, 65, 66, 67, 68, 70, 71, 72, 76, 78, 85, 90
    discontinuous 80
    erratic 78
wool 12, 22, 31, 40, 46, 48, 60, 78, 79, 82, 83, 84, 85, 90
wrapping 11, 15, 18, 22, 24, 30, 34, 37, 38, 44, 48, 49, 50, 52, 60, 64, 68, 69, 73, 83, 89, 90, 92, 95

yarns 9, 11, 12, 22, 23, 30, 32, 33, 38, 40, 44, 46, 47, 48, 50, 56, 62, 63, 64, 65, 66, 68, 69, 70, 71, 75, 76, 83, 84, 86, 87, 89, 90 *see also* names of individual yarns
    animal (protein), 40, 46
    plant (cellulose) 40
    synthetic 40